Forty Years a Gambler

Ian Douglas Bartlett

Prologue

It seemed as though I was a spectator at a wrestling match where one opponent just couldn't seem to hold the other down for the count of three. In reality I was appearing for the third time in The Crown Court watching the prosecutor and defence barristers argue over some point of law, each giving way to the other in a performance that would have been fitting in any drama. When they had finished they sat down.

Then the judge looked straight at me and said "Bail denied."

I was led down to the court cells, which are no bigger than your average bathroom. They certainly do not come with a view and they usually smell of stale urine. The hotter the day; the stronger the smell. The plastic containers of food are served up straight from the microwave. If you ask for sausage, mash and peas, you get cat meat (and even then I am doing it a service by calling it that).

It was a short twenty minute van journey to the prison. As we arrived, the big outer gates of the prison were opened. The van stopped between the outer and inner gates and the engine was turned off. The outer gate was closed, then the security guard got off the van and handed all of the Court's paperwork over. Once security were happy we were escorted one by one into the prison reception where we were greeted by prison officers making the usual comments like "Nice to see you back," and "Welcome home." We were each then strip searched with the mandatory bend-over-and-touch-your-toes routine. This was done to make sure that nothing was being smuggled back in to prison, but it felt more like an exercise in humiliation. All of our personal property was placed in sealed plastic bags and locked away.

Then we were allocated our wings and cells in the main prison. As I was being escorted along the corridors to the wings I could hear the alarm bells going; some disturbance had kicked off, maybe fighting between inmates. That kind of thing could literally start over the most petty disagreements, or just people falling out because they're from different parts of the country. After the bells had stopped ringing we arrived on our wing and were sent straight to our cell. The door was opened just long enough to shut with me on the other side, and that was it.

Now, in the cell was a man who I'd never met. His behaviour suggested he may have had a mental illness, or perhaps he was coming down from drugs. It's hard to tell, but I knew I was faced with a person around whom I had to act cautiously. After the pleasantries were over it was a case of watching my back. Once you are locked in the cell at night, it is very rare that the prison officers on duty will open the cell door, even in an emergency. If a fight occurs the usual response is that there are not enough members of staff on duty and you will have to wait until the morning. It is best that you try to get on with your cellmate.

The prison has a set routine for meals and association, which are always at set times. Association times are when prisoners are let out of their cells between the hours of 7pm and 8:30pm. This time is usually spent playing pool or table tennis, or visiting other inmates on the wing. This typically happens three nights per week.

There is always the threat of violence, and you have to watch your back at all times. At no point can you ever show weakness; if you do there are people ready to take advantage. I was lucky; I always stood my ground and I made friends with a lot of otherwise potentially dangerous people.

***

As I lay on my bed three months later, I could hear the shouts and screams echoing across the prison courtyard again. "Nothing out of the ordinary," I thought to myself. "Probably just another row over alcohol or drugs." I concluded that it was of no concern of mine, and so the clamour faded to the back of my mind to be replaced by my many worries, and eventually by another uncomfortable sleep.

It was five in the morning when I heard the jangling of keys. I could hear the prison officer approaching, the unmistakeable sound of keys echoing across the wing as his footsteps got nearer. I knew he was now at my cell door. He turned the lock and the door flew open. "Get your kit!" his voice bellowed. He was a huge man of at least 6ft 4, and weighing in at what must have been about 18 stone, he was not someone you would not like to meet in a dark alley. His booming voice had hardly finished echoing around the walls before I was up - kit swung over my shoulder – and out of the cell.

The night before going out of prison (whatever the reason) you mull things over in your mind. You picture yourself at court, and think about the different outcomes – maybe even a "Not guilty." For me, this was just a fantasy, but there was no chance I would be sleeping that night, so I was up and prepared and waiting for the cell door to open.

I closed the door behind me, and as we walked along the wing corridor I could hear the murmurings coming from the cells. It was alright for them; they still had another two hours' sleep. As I was escorted along the prison corridors more men began to join me from the other wings. All of us were heading in the same direction: The Crown Court. This was the day of the sentencing.

After we all entered the reception area, we were called one by one into a small room and ordered to strip naked. "Anything that can be smuggled into prison can be smuggled out. Drugs, money, alcohol, tobacco." They weren't taking any risks. Once the search was conducted we were given back our civilian clothes.

'The sweatbox' is the name affectionately given to the van which takes people from the prison gate to the Crown Court. It allowed each person a space of about six feet upwards by two feet wide. Our trip was only twenty minutes, but some have to travel like this for hours, moving across the entire country. There are no toilets, only paper cups. Before we knew it the journey was over and I was in the cells below the court. My barrister came in, but I knew the whole thing was a foregone conclusion; all of the talking had already taken place over the course of the last three months. The police, the prosecutor, the defence and the judge had all come to an agreement beforehand, and I had long since resigned myself to the inevitable.

The court proceedings went by so quickly I felt that I was in a whirlwind, not really comprehending what was going on. At the same time I knew the ins and outs of the situation. Is this the mechanism that the human mind resorts to when faced with a head on car crash? It certainly felt like that to me.

As I was called to Court 1 and escorted to the dock a single thought crossed my mind: "What have I done?" Suddenly I was the centre of attention; alone in front of so many faces, none of them familiar. My so called 'mates' had all deserted me. As I looked around me I saw a sea of expressionless faces. For one brief moment it felt as if it was not me standing in the dock; surely it was someone else. How did I get here?

The process was clinical. The charges were read out. All that remained was for the judge to look straight at me and pronounce sentence.

Childhood

I was the eldest of three children. I had a brother Neil and a sister Margaret, and we lived with my mother (also named Margaret) and Peter, my father. My father and Mother met each other whilst serving in the R.A.F, but I have little memory of that era.

One of my earliest memories was of visiting my grandparents in Sunderland, and my granddad taking me to see Sunderland play a night game at Roker Park. He lifted me on his shoulders so I could see the game. I remember the mist coming in from the North Sea, and how when the ball was at the opposite end of the ground I could hardly see anything, so I had to rely on the noise that came from the crowd to determine whether we had scored. This certainly was a fond memory for me and I have been a Sunderland supporter ever since, although I must admit supporting the club tends to bring more pain than joy.

On another occasion I remember that we had to visit Sunderland as my granddad had died. I was very upset and I recall that the coffin containing him was placed in the living room of his house and I was told that I had to look at him before he was buried the next day. Reluctantly I approached the coffin. I was absolutely petrified and as I looked into the open coffin I could see his lifeless face drained of all emotion; his body an empty shell. This picture of him stayed with me for quite a while.

And so it was just the five of us, and life when I was a child wasn't easy. I was forced to wear shorts even in the depths of winter. I would run home from school absolutely frozen and the first thing I would do is put my hands in front of the coal fire. Mum would try to warn me - "Don't do that, you'll get chilblains." Mums know best, and she was right; the feeling of my hands thawing bit far worse than the cold.

Even at a young age I felt a sense of responsibility for my younger siblings. Being the eldest child brings responsibilities; I felt as though I had to protect them, especially if they were being picked on by other children. It didn't help that our father seemed absent for much of my childhood. I often thought that he must be working and it was my responsibility to take care of the young ones until he got home from work. When he returned home he would always look to see if we had done our homework. Pythagoras's theory was a particular sore point; I always got it wrong and I still do, but because he had a degree in mathematics he expected me to have his level of understanding. Bed time every night was 6pm. As a young child I remember looking out of my bedroom window wishing that I could be out playing like the other children.

We were living in a three bedroom terraced house and there was very little money for heating up the home. Many a night we were huddled in the living room on the sofa trying to keep warm. Often the electricity was cut off because the bills were not paid, and we had to see by candlelight. The best thing to do was go to bed early and get under the blankets, hoping that they would keep me warm. But often I would wake up in the night and see my own breath.

To the best of my knowledge everything was fine in our family. It wasn't the most comfortable of lives, but it was what I knew. Then my dad made an announcement. We were moving to a place in Cumbria called Brampton. I tried to stop the move from happening. What about my mates? What about my school? But no matter what I had to say, his mind was made up. We were going.

My initial feelings were mixed. First there was a real sense of bewilderment, and then sadness at the thought of having to move away. Eventually that gave way to resignation that I could not control the chain of events. It was out of my hands. We moved into a nice little three bedroom house right next to a playing field with some swings to play on. My dad seemed happier here, although I suspected the pub might have had something to do with it. He always seemed to be there.

On one occasion we were sitting around the kitchen table eagerly awaiting some delicious trifle. My favourite! I looked over to see that my brother had been given a much bigger bowl than me. Naturally I complained, and my mother must have just snapped. She threw a kitchen fork in my general direction, but her aim wasn't general enough and it stuck into the side of my head. I screamed, and she tried to say sorry, but there was nothing else for it; the doctor had to be called. Blood was pouring down my face, and when he arrived he took one startled look at me and said "How did you do that, Ian?" I looked at him, and then I looked at my mother. "I fell down the stairs, and landed on the fork" was my unconvincing reply. Surely he wouldn't believe it? He looked at me again, paused, and then proceeded to patch up my head without another word on the subject. After he had left, my mother was full of remorse, so I ended up with another bowl of trifle much bigger than my brother's. I had learnt that lying was not only ok, but that it worked.

One Saturday afternoon we were sitting in the living room watching TV. The horse racing was on, and on this particular occasion my dad asked me whether I'd like to have a go on the horses. I was ecstatic; a chance to spend quality time with my dad was too good an opportunity to miss. So it became a regular occurrence - every Saturday I would bet my pocket money on the horse racing. I lost nearly every time. If only I'd figured out at that point that gamblers rarely win. I recall one particular race vividly. My horse had just jumped the last fence, well clear of its nearest rival. Then, unprompted my dad switched channels. Ten minutes later he switched back, but by then the coverage had moved on and he informed me that my horse had lost. Then the penny dropped; he had no money and was taking mine. I was betting against my father with my pocket money, and he was willing to take it from me. He had lost all of *his* money that morning at the bookmakers.

Another time he had promised me that he would take me and my friends to the circus. I remember him coming across the field on a Friday afternoon. Pay day. He stopped in front of us and said that if any boy could find his wage packet on the field they would receive a five pound reward. My mates took off running all over the place. I stayed rooted to the spot. I knew where the money had gone. He hadn't lost it; he'd gambled it. I started to develop an uncanny way of being able to pick up on when my dad was trying to cover his tracks.

By now there was constant friction between my parents, and I heard everything. The shouting, screaming and slamming of doors were all crystal clear. I escaped sometimes by putting a pillowcase over my ears to block out the world around me. That was my survival mechanism.

My dad's luck didn't improve. He came back one night with a greyhound that he had won in a card game. He was named Rip, and, true to his name he didn't last long. Half way through his first race his heart gave up and he dropped dead. My dad dragged him off into the woods to bury him. Rest In Peace Rip. Dad seemed to do everything himself. Even when he was playing cards well into almost every night, and it was clear he had a problem, he never sought help. In those days you didn't. It was part of 'being a man.'

Then one day I was playing upstairs with Neil and there was a loud knock at the door. It was the Police asking for Peter Bartlett. My mum didn't try to stop it; they just took him away. We were ushered into our bedrooms and told nothing. It was only much later on that I found out that my dad had had a part time job at an electrician's shop, which just happened to be next door to the bookmakers. The till had been cleared out. He'd had the lot. My mum said he'd gone on holiday. I wish she'd told the truth. But, as quickly as he was gone he returned with an announcement. We were moving to Scotland.

I was angry. Angry that I would be separated from my friends again, and angry that I'd lose everything my home gave me. Football on the field. Skimming stones on the water. Climbing trees. All of that would be lost, and all I could do about it was to slam my bedroom door in frustration. I withdrew into myself and distanced myself from those around me. I was becoming more and more isolated.

A removal van arrived and we were in Scotland by the end of the week. Being an English kid in a Scottish school was not a good position to find myself in, and I was often getting into fights. I remember one day my brother and I were at the back of the house playing, and as the game became more heated we began to swear at each other. Unknown to us the back door of the house was open and my dad was listening to every word that we were saying. Suddenly we saw him and immediately we stopped swearing as if nothing had happened. He looked at us and said calmly "You two. Up here now." I don't know about Neil's, but my mouth suddenly became dry and my legs began to shake. As we entered the kitchen we said nothing. Then dad said "I have just heard you both swearing, and I have told you many times before not to. But, I do know that I have brought up two intelligent young boys, so I am going to punish you, but I am going to give you a *choice* of punishment. I want you to discuss between yourselves what you are going to do. It's either going to be my hand across your backside, or a book, or this broom stick. Now go into the corner and when you have made your decision tell me." We discussed our options and it was a no brainer, the hand would sting and the broom would hurt us badly, so the safe and obvious option was the book. This certainly would not hurt as much as the other two, and so we agreed that the book was our choice. When we announced our decision I could see a smile stretch across my father's face. "That's a good choice. I am so glad that I am bringing up two intelligent boys." At this stage we thought we had got away with it lightly. Then came the remainder of his sentence... "however, I will not tolerate swearing and you are both going to get the broom. He made us lean over a chair. When he wacked Neil he jumped up like a cat on a hot tin roof. Then it was my turn, and I vainly put my hands across my backside to soften the blow. Unfortunately it didn't work, and I too jumped up, yelping with pain. We certainly did not swear again (well, not within ear shot of my dad.)

When I arrived home one evening there was a purple chopper waiting. My dad had won big at the bookies, and he must have felt guilty for something because I got the bike that he'd bought with his winnings. I used to play on that bike whenever I could. It had 3 gears which I would use my hand to change, which were situated between my legs, but I was warned not to go on the road. And would you believe it, the one time I took the bike on the road I caught the sight of my dad out of the corner of my eye and fell in the middle of the road. The next thing I heard was "Ian get in the house now!" Another beating took place and the bike was confiscated.

My dad seemed to be around less and less; his gambling and drinking were tearing the family apart by this point. Then, one day, he was gone. It wasn't until later that I found out that it wasn't only his friends he was meeting. I was too young to really understand the implications of a married person having an affair. I would learn that people start talking, word gets around, and it's those without a voice who receive the greatest impact. People start to do things you didn't know they were capable of, and victims are created. My mum had discovered he was seeing another woman, and kicked him out. I was nine years old, and to this day, forty years later, I have only ever seen him once. Here was the evidence, right in front of me, that gambling and alcohol have the power to ruin lives. But I had other things to focus on. As far as I could tell I needed to become the bread winner. I came to this conclusion at the age of nine.

My mum had started to date different men, and I disliked each and every one of them. No one could take the place of my own father. One of the men that she dated was called Vince. He was, in my opinion, not a good role model for any child to look up to. He used to go around the house showing us karate moves, and he constantly informed us that he was a black belt. I thought "Yeah the only black belt that you hold is the black belt to hold your trousers up with," but I kept this to myself. He also showed me where I could steal potatoes at night, and to watch out for the farmer. We filled our sacks up and returned home. When he left my mum I then had the knowledge that he had shown me, so I would go out and apply it.

I would leave the house when it got dark, and with a little torch by my side make my way across the main road and up a hill to the farmers' fields. The potatoes were ready for the harvest, and I used to crawl under the fence, pull up the potatoes and stuff them into a plastic bag. Only when it was full I would make my way home. I would do this at least once a week. When the other children my age were tucked up in bed asleep I was out in the dark stealing. We needed to eat.

Then another man came on to the scene, and he treated us terribly. He would think nothing of hitting myself or Neil, and it was only much later that I learnt that he had once battered my brother for two hours. I still can't know how he must have felt for all that time.

He started to hit my mother, with me in the living watching. I ran straight across and got between them. He dragged me down the hallway by my hair and hit me. I showed no emotion, but I told myself that when I was older I would come and pay him back for what he was doing. I was ten – revenge shouldn't have been on my radar.

Payback came sooner than I could have ever imagined: within a matter of weeks. My mother was, as usual, short of money, and one day she asked me to go down to the train station where her boyfriend worked to get some from him. When he saw me he invited me in to sit down, so I took a seat on a wooden chair. It was at this point that an opportunity presented itself. He had turned his back to talk to somebody when I noticed that the small wooden drawer containing all of the money had been left open. Wasting no time, I whipped my hand into the drawer and withdrew ten pounds. He turned back around. Had I been caught?

"Here's a pound for your mother, now get out!"

I did, and very quickly at that. I walked home laughing my head off; I knew he would get into trouble for this, and sure enough, later that evening I heard him telling my mother that he had been suspended. I had to bury my face in a pillow to stop my laughter being heard. I still can't believe he never put two and two together. There are plenty of ways to skin a cat. As a result of this he lost his job and a little later the relationship between my mother and him ended.

My mum began to see this friend, and one day as I went into the living room they had out in front of them on the coffee table the letters A-Z and a few numbers. They were breathing into a glass and putting it on the table, and then they put their fingertips on the glass and asked questions. The glass began to move and I was afraid. I ran out of the room that time, but later on that week I joined in, and I remember feeling confused, but I didn't want to argue so I breathed into the glass. When I put my fingertip on the rim with my mum she began asking questions like "Where is Ian's dad living?" The glass moved around the table incredibly fast; I was sure my mum was pushing it along, and she was sure that it was me. But it was neither of us, and when I quickly pulled my finger off the glass it stopped straight away. I told my mum I did not want to do that anymore but later on the following week I could hear people in the living room whilst I was in bed and they were doing the same thing. That night I slept uneasily.

Teenage Years

There was excitement in our house. The unthinkable had happened; my mother had found out where my dad was living, and what was even more astonishing was that he was willing to meet us, his children. I could hardly sleep in the week leading up to being reunited with him. My brother, my sister and I couldn't stop talking about it; we were all so excited.

I don't know how my mother had managed to find him, but she had, and at that moment in time that was all that mattered. The arrangements were made, and on the morning of our visit we made sure that we were scrubbed clean. As we hopped into the car that was to transport us to his house we must have looked like three little angels (this couldn't be further from the truth.) My mother was not present, so one of her friends drove us to a place called Livingston in Lothian, Scotland. The car journey seemed to take at least a day in my world, but in reality we arrived at his house three hours later.

The excitement was unbearable - this was the first time we had met him since he walked out three years previously. As the car pulled up outside his house I was utterly amazed at the sight of a big garden with a car in the driveway. This house looked like a mansion, and there he was standing in the doorway ushering us in. I hugged him. It felt odd, like I was hugging a stranger for the first time. My brother and sister were less reserved, running and jumping into his arms. Then we were introduced to his wife and our new step sisters. There was so much to take in.

We all sat around the kitchen table and we were given a glass of lemonade each and a bite to eat. His wife seemed nice enough but she said very little. She seemed to be content just watching the proceedings unfold and her daughters just stared at us and looked a bit lost, as if they didn't really understand what was going on.

My dad had mentioned that he'd had all of his teeth taken out because of a disease in his gums, and I thought he would not be able to chew on his favourite meal: roast beef with Yorkshire pudding. A Sunday roast was, from what I can remember, his favourite meal. He then said to us that he was going to take us to the shops and we could have whatever we wanted, and I remember that I got a Liverpool shirt. To my utter dismay there were no Sunderland shirts. Neil got a Celtic top and Margaret a doll and there seemed to be very little conversation going on. As I walked behind my dad, Neil and Margaret were holding his hands. I was thinking "If only it could always be like this." And at that very moment I began to realise just how much I had missed my dad.

Unfortunately the visit was over in a blink of an eye, and as we all stood on his doorstep ready to depart I had a feeling of grief. Of course I kept those feelings to myself. My brother and sister were not quite so stoic. In floods of tears, and with an extreme reluctance to leave they had to be prised away from my father's arms. I helped with this procedure and we eventually bundled into the car.

On the journey home I reassured the young ones that everything would be alright and that they would be visiting dad sooner than they thought, and Margaret said with excitement in her voice "Like next week, Ian? "I replied that we would, of course, which seemed to settle her down a little, but Neil didn't say a word.

Before we knew it we were back home. Mum immediately began to ask all manner of different questions: "What's his wife like? Has he invited you back? What's his house like?" The questions seemed endless. I tried to answer them, but we were all exhausted and I collapsed into bed that night with lots of doubts of my own going through my mind. "Why did he leave us? Would we get to stay with him now?" And with those questions spinning round and round I fell asleep.

About a week after we had all returned home I noticed that Neil had been out all day. I asked my mum where he was, but she seemed guarded with her response. She told me that he was at the swimming pool, which I didn't believe because we never went to the swimming pool. Why would Neil be there? Later on he appeared and said absolutely nothing to me, which was very strange, but I kept my thoughts to myself. A month later Neil had disappeared again, which was even more bizarre, and this time when I confronted my mum the answer I received shook me completely. "Neil has gone to live with your father and you won't see either of them again."

She sat me down and said that Neil had run away twice and was picked up by the police wandering across the Forth Road Bridge. He had been making his way to be with his father and now my father was going to take him to live with him. I was devastated. Not only had I lost my father, but now my brother had also abandoned us. It all seemed so much to bear, and the questions came flooding in: "Why can't I live with my dad? Does he not love me?"

I was totally confused and bewildered, and for the next month I walked around in a complete daze. But I found resolve from somewhere, and I kept going. I just told myself this was how things were meant to be.

The next four years took their toll on my mum. There were three suicide attempts, all of which involved sleeping pills and alcohol. These were a clear call for help. She was trying to cope with two children who were growing up fast, and each one of us must have been hard to handle in our own way. Her various partners failed to help, and I believe some made things worse. I can only assume that her situation was unbearable, and her cries were heard by Social Services. I do believe that she received help through social workers and I even remember one whose name was Nan. She was a gentle soul who would often come around and give advice to my mum, even at weekends. This woman also befriended my sister, and I know that Margaret loved her; she was such a positive influence on the family.

My behaviour was going downhill quickly, to the point where I was sent to spend a week with my mum's friends Valerie and Jock, and their three daughters. Valerie and Jock lived ten minutes from our house and Valerie would often pop in for a cup of coffee and a talk with my mum. They frequently went out together to play bingo, and she would bring her daughters to our house and they would play endless games with Margaret. I can't remember their names but what I do remember is that they were loud; I would hear ear piercing screams that only girls can make that would go right through me. They would often ask me to join in with their games, but being a young man I felt that the only proper reply was a stout "No way." I was more concerned with kicking a football in the park or playing Action Man games. No chance of getting me to play girl games. Perish the thought.

Jock worked in the local shipyard and from what I can remember of him is, he provided for his family and loved and cared for them. What I was soon to discover was that he also had a temper; I certainly knew where I stood with him. He was the type that if he told you to do anything you would do it. At that point that is really what I needed.

Even though it was only a week, it gave me a glimpse into another life: one with routine, reliability and people who truly cared for me. The carpets were new and clean, the fridge was stocked with delicious food and everything was organised. I knew when the meals were coming, and I knew when I had to be in bed. They both seemed happy and I can remember being tucked up in bed feeling warm and secure, grateful for a full stomach and two people who seemed to care for my welfare. I can remember their laughter coming from the living room. This was something that I was not used to. The girls had settled down in their rooms and everything seemed fine, and for a brief moment I felt content. The week was over too quickly for me and I was returned home with a warning to behave myself from both of them. The routine is something I really enjoyed, and I was sad to be leaving.

About a week later, I was sitting in the living room having my dinner when there was a knock at the front door. My mum got up and answered the door, and a man introduced himself as a reporter from The Sun. He then proceeded to ask whether we had any pictures of Jock or Valerie. This immediately got my attention because it was such a strange question. My mum replied saying that she hadn't, and I didn't think about it anymore. Then, a few weeks later, I learnt from her that Jock had caught Valerie having an affair, and had cornered her and stabbed her over seventy times. She had died in hospital from her injuries. Jock got life in prison, and the three girls were taken in by relatives.

While all of this was sinking in, break-ins became frequent in our house. We were barricading the back door against intruders, using furniture, but it didn't do much good. Our house was the last in the row, and the back garden led onto wasteland. There were no lights, so we were an easy target. That's something you can understand clearly as a child, and we were frightened. I tried to hide it by standing up for the rest of my family; I felt as though I was now the man of the house.

One night I was awoken by strange voices. I got up to investigate and found two men standing over my mum's bed. My mum seemed far beyond drunk; I had never seen anyone in so bad a condition. I had no time to think through the situation that I was now faced with so natural instinct took over. I had stumbled upon a scene that was beyond my comprehension; I looked at my mum again and it looked like she was near death so I quickly ran in my pyjamas to the phone box, rain and tears pouring down my face. I screamed down the phone for an ambulance, and by the time I had run back home again I could see the flashing lights. Just as I arrived at the front door my mum was wheeled past me, unconscious, with an oxygen mask over her face. She was quickly put in the ambulance and it sped away. I was taken into the living room and I remember a police woman telling me that everything would be okay. They arranged that we would stay with neighbours overnight while the men who were in the house were being questioned, and not for the first time I was alone. I was to learn later that my mum had taken a concoction of sleeping pills and alcohol. The next morning I was in foster care and Margaret had been taken away and placed with another family. We were all separated again.

I was picked up and ushered into a waiting car by a social worker. It felt as if we were on the road for at least four hours. I didn't know where I was going. I didn't know what was happening. I just felt as though everything was spiralling out of control.

It wasn't until the car stopped that the reality of what was happening struck me. But instead of the dread I was expecting to feel, there was warmth. I looked up from where we had stopped and saw in front of me a big farmhouse. My eyes nearly popped out of their sockets. As we pulled up to this farm there were hens running around and dogs barking. I got out of the car and could taste the fresh country air (including a noticeable whiff of cow dung.)

A woman and a man came out of the farmhouse to greet me. They looked like my idea of typical farmers. The woman wore a flowery dress and I noticed that she had big hands and a warm smile, and the man was wearing old mucky trousers and a baggy jumper. His hands looked rough and dirty, and he just had a look that said "Welcome." The dogs were barking and wagging their tails; it felt like there was a chorus of voices that were happy I had arrived. Then the woman smothered me in her arms and I felt as though I was going to burst. I had not felt like this in a very long time; the idea of being loved unconditionally was incredible. It got better when I walked through the front door and my eyes came to rest on the large plate of scones with butter, jam and cream sitting on the kitchen table. My coat was taken and I made a beeline straight for them. I began demolishing them.

"Would you like a scone?" the woman asked.

By then I had made a serious dent in the pile, and within ten minutes they were gone.

"Would you like some more?"

I didn't say no. I was a bit more reserved this time though, first eating the extra scones (with more care than the first lot) and then delicately removing the crumbs and jam that I had smeared all over my face. Glorious. After I had finished, we went into the living room, which had a great big coal fire. I took a seat right next to the source of the heat, and as I was slowly drifting off to sleep, I was picked up by the man and taken to my bed. 'This is the life,' I thought. 'It doesn't get any better than this!" And with that thought, and with a full stomach, I slept, smiling like a Cheshire Cat. I was awoken the next morning by the sound of a cockerel.

A new home meant a new school. I particularly remember that school for its milk. It came in a bottle at ten each morning, lukewarm because they used to leave it by the radiator for some reason. Another clear memory I have is of the school fete. I made a robot costume out of cardboard and entered it into a competition. I remember that when I paraded in front of the judges my cardboard hat swivelled around and I couldn't see when I was going. Apparently if I hadn't been stopped I was in danger of being judged in the 'sheep' category, but a kind member of the public set me on course, and I made it to where I should have been. I received third prize and a sixpence. I was smiling all day long.

I would get up at six each morning to be taken out onto the fields with the farmer to go and check the cattle and sheep. It was always cold that time of morning but the farmer's wife wrapped me up well. I would look up at the sunrise on those mornings, and seeing the red-tinted sky with the mist lifting up from the land, and feeling the warmth of the sun take a hold filled me with a sense of wonder. The beauty of getting up at that time was that when we returned to the farmhouse and were greeted with a loving hug, there was still time for a hearty breakfast of bacon, eggs and sausages. Then it was off to school, or piano lessons and games at weekends.

At night time I was responsible for putting the hens away, and I was to ensure that they were locked up, safe from the prying eyes of foxes. I can tell you, most nights I would lie awake checking in my head whether I'd remembered that evening. The slightest noise would make me start, but I always managed to reassure myself that I'd remembered, and that they were safe, and the warmth of the bed convinced me that I was going to stay exactly where I was, at least until the morning.

Then, as quickly as my new life had begun, I was torn away from foster parents. The news arrived, I hugged and kissed them with tears running down my face, and with a sadness I can't describe, I was placed in a car and taken home to my mum.

As the car pulled up outside the house I was greeted by my mother.

"Are you ok?" she asked.

"Yes." I replied.

That was it. No kiss. No hug. I had arrived back home. The house was cold, and I remember rolling up pieces of newspaper and gathering chunks of wood, and trying to get the coal fire going. We spent many a night huddled in front of that fire just trying to keep ourselves warm. There never seemed to be much food in the house so I used to go down to the seafront, which was a minute's walk, and when the tide was out I collected winkles. I used to put a lot of effort into collecting those crustaceans. Once I'd got enough, I put them into a pot of boiling water, waited for about five minutes, and then proceeded to remove the edible parts from the shell with a needle. It would take at least a pot-full to even dent the hunger pains.

Then there were the three day power cuts. We never seemed to have any electricity in the house, so we used to use candles to see. Sometimes the only way to keep warm was to just go to bed. I could often see my own breath indoors, and when I breathed on the inside of the windows ice had formed. It was not my mother's fault though; this was just the set of circumstances that we faced each and every day.

It was when I was nearing sixteen that I decided to get away, so I applied to join the RAF. In all honesty I didn't care what I did; I just needed to leave the cycle of hunger and cold behind. I enquired at the RAF careers office in Dundee about joining, and the sergeant gave a good presentation. He said they were short of stewards, and I needed no further encouragement. I took the entrance exam three months later, and within a further month I received a letter saying that I had passed. I then went back to Dundee, and along with two others I swore allegiance to Queen and Country, and in a matter of days I was on a train to RAF Swinderby for basic training.

My mother saw me off at the train station. There was no visible emotion from her, and I was glad just to be getting away from the set of circumstances I had been in. As the train was leaving the platform I could see my mother walking away. There was no wave or backward glance. I was by myself again.

The RAF and Military Prison

I was so excited! I had a travel warrant in my hand and I was headed for RAF Swinderby for seven weeks of basic training. The journey down wasn't too much of a strain; it was catered, and I even considered buying a beer, but I thought better of it. I was about to serve in the military after all. As I looked out of the window I was surprised to see so much open space and green land after living on cramped council estates for most of my life. These scenes were new to me, and the journey passed by in no time at all. The train pulled up at the station, and as I stepped off I heard a voice shouting "You lot, over here!" We must have stuck out like sore thumbs with our bags slung over our shoulders, and there, standing in his uniform was an RAF sergeant. He was a big stocky man with an unmistakable scouse accent. He looked like he had gone twelve rounds with Muhammad Ali and had somehow come out the other end to tell the tale. Under his arm was what looked like a baton that he was using with some effect to round up the entire group. He was like a shepherd rounding up his sheep.

We were all ushered onto a bus. There must have been at least twenty of us and we were all from different parts of the country. There was Jock; a Scottish lad who seemed no older than me. He seemed pleasant enough, from the courteous "Hello" he used to introduce himself to me. We seemed to bond immediately, partly because we had both come down from Scotland, and partly because we were both so young, so we leaned on each other for support and friendship. Then there was Scouse Dave. He was a lot older; I would say he looked at least twenty-five. I could hardly understand him through his thick accent, and I think that the feeling was mutual! It seemed to me that he was speaking a foreign language and I was always asking him "What did you say?" and I am sure this irritated him. And then there was Cockney Luke. He was a real laugh; always coming up with jokes that would have the rest of us on our knees roaring with laughter. You could say that we were a real mix of what Britain had to offer, and I am sure that was much to the dismay of any casual onlooker who might have happened to pop their head round the door.

As the bus started on its journey to the base I had no idea what awaited us all. We had assembled from all around the country to train together in the coming weeks. The first step was to be led to an RAF supply store to be measured up and issued with uniforms. Not many of us knew our own sizes. The storehouse corporal said "Neck" and I started to put my hand on my neck to see if there was something on it that I had missed. Maybe I had forgotten to wash and there was visible dirt on my neck? Then all of a sudden this man produced a foghorn voice: "You *stupid* little idiot I want your neck size! Now you're feeling your neck like you're about to strangle yourself. I'll do it for you in a minute. What's your neck size?" I replied that I didn't know, and with that he lent across the counter and nearly *did* strangle me with the tape measure. He shouted "sixteen and a half" and I could hear laughter coming from down the line as the other recruits witnessed the unfolding farce. The corporal seemed to erupt like a volcano; I'm I could see hot steaming lava coming out of his mouth. "Get them all out on to the yard!" he screamed, and with that we were doing press ups and sit-ups and running on the spot. This was a stark warning to do exactly what we were told and act sensibly. They were not going to put up with anyone messing about. After we had all finished the exercises we were marched back into the storehouse, where this time everyone was silent and we did exactly what we were told. We all received our kits, which comprised of shoes, plimsolls, socks, underwear, trousers, shorts, shirts, tee-shirts, ties, jumpers, a beret and bedding.

During that first day I tried to take in as much as I could. Jock and I were in the same billet but Luke and Dave had been assigned another. At least I had made friends with Jock; over the coming seven weeks we would spend most of the time together. The sleeping arrangements were basic: a single bed in a billet with twelve other men. This seven week period was all about discipline. We were up at 6am each day and it was drill, drill and more drill. We were also taught basic skills such as ironing, boot-polishing, and (for some people) shaving! There are always individuals who tried to take the lead, or even bully, where twelve to twenty men are in a billet together. Some had been there longer than others, and on more than one occasion, after lights-out 'The Initiation Gang' came round. They would pull unsuspecting residents out of their beds and shove them under the cold shower. They would force them to do sit-ups, and then they would cover them in black boot polish. They thought this was hilarious, and in their warped minds with their distorted senses of humour this is what made them men. When they came after me one night I was having none of it. With fists clenched I assured them that if they tried anything I'd smash their faces in, and with that they retreated and picked on a young lad two beds down. Three nights later they picked on Jock. I quickly jumped out of my bed and with fists ready advanced towards the gang that was now trying to attack my new-found mate. Jock jumped out of his bed, shouting "You will have me and Ian to answer to now!" This seemed to do the trick, and they retreated yet again to pick on someone else. Throughout the training this kind of bullying was rife, and it seemed that the corporals and sergeants condoned it. Perhaps they were in agreement that this treatment really did build character. One of our training exercises was a ten mile hike. The rules stated that if anyone was left behind, everyone was forced to march double time until the straggler caught up. That individual was then picked on for some time afterwards.

Another part of our training was in biological and chemical warfare, which taught us how to operate while under gas attack. We were issued a gas mask and put in a concrete bunker. A canister of gas was released, and then we had to take our masks off and yell "Gas! Gas!" before counting to sixty, putting the mask on and scrambling out of the bunker. The lads were coughing and spluttering with tears streaming down their faces; all except one. There was one man who had none of the symptoms the rest of us had. Curious, I asked him what made him different. He replied that he was from Northern Ireland and had to put up with canisters of gas going off constantly. This made sense to me at the time.

In all training military establishments one is awoken early in the morning. For us this meant a 6am start. Our alarm was the corporal turning on the lights and shouting his head off. "You lot get out of your beds! You then have twenty minutes to shower and shave and to arrange all of your bedding immaculately presented on top of your bed and all of your kit folded neatly in your wardrobe!" Now, there is a correct way to fold these items and you are shown how to do this in week one of your training. If you don't fold it in the way that you have been shown there are consequences. An example of this was when one morning my kit wasn't how it should have been, and the response from the corporal was to upend my bed and pull down the wardrobe. Everything I owned was scattered over the billet floor. Not content with this he pressed his face into mine and shouted so loud that I thought he would burst my ear drums. Now my reaction to this might seem strange, but for whatever reason in situations like this I feel a sudden urge to laugh. I bit the insides of my cheeks. As you can imagine if this had failed I'd have been in big trouble for undermining authority. Luckily I was able to hold back long enough for the situation to pass by.

Once the early morning inspection was over and we'd had breakfast we were ordered onto the parade ground. The majority of each day was taken up by marching. I can hear the echoing of the sergeant major's orders even now: "Left, right, left, right, about turn, quick march!" and the endless shouting that accompanies the orders: "You stupid little man; don't you know the difference between left and right, and who put your tie on this morning? Your mother's not here now. Get it sorted right now!" And as the unfortunate individual was enduring this everyone else would have to endure double time, which was marching up and down on the spot. It goes without saying that whoever had caused this tiring task to be inflicted would get even more abuse from his colleagues. After at least three hours of drill we were marched to the canteen and given lunch. Now the meals were always good, and we had plenty to choose from. The saying says that an army marches on its stomach, and that was certainly true for us. The canteen was huge; big enough to cater for at least a thousand men, and the meal times were always at a set time. This was a good time to talk about home and who we were missing and what we would do when the training was over. Letters were always eagerly anticipated, if only to keep us informed of what was happening in the outside world.

After Lunch we were taught life skills in a classroom environment. These classes included how to do the ironing, polish your shoes and even sewing. They are skills that are essential in the military, and pretty useful in the outside world. They made it clear what the RAF was expecting from us, and that was cleanliness and tidiness, with polished shoes and shirts and uniforms ironed. These lessons would last for about an hour and we would have three per week.

Then came the fitness work: assault courses, long runs and gym training. In the early sessions many of us were physically sick. After all, not many of us were fit; definitely not as fit as the RAF required, and as a consequence we often went on ten mile at the double hikes through the countryside with our kit bags full. Up hills and down hills the green countryside was beautiful. I saw a lot of the grass and dirt pretty close up, often with my face pressed into it after recovering from a gruelling hike. I just collapsed into a heap but I was encouraged not to remain there for long. A reassuring hand would haul me to my feet, and a bellowing in my ear that I hadn't finished yet would remind me to carry on.

At around 5pm we had our dinner, and the evenings were mostly spent cleaning the washrooms and floors of our billets. They had to be perfect for the morning inspection, and of course we had to make sure that in our own personal bed space our kit was clean and ready. By the end of each day we collapsed into our beds, and at 10pm the lights were turned off and the next thing we were aware of was that all too familiar voice of our corporal: "Get out of your beds you lot!"

The days passed like this until the time came for our Passing Out Parade. We were all dressed in the Number One Uniform. This uniform was our best kit, which we would only use for parades with our shoes polished so well we could see our faces in them. Then we were paraded in front of the group captain. This was the first time that I had ever seen the camp commander; the man responsible for the smooth running of the base. There were lots of families present who had travelled from all over the country to watch the parade. It was a hot summer's day and everything seemed to be going smoothly, and suddenly I saw one man fall straight onto the concrete. He was quickly lifted up and taken away by the medics, and then I saw another man fall and the same happened to him. The heat had been too much, and the standing still at attention had made things worse, but all the endless drill that we had endured over the previous seven weeks had paid off for most of us. The rest of the parade ran smoothly, and we all had passed basic training. I congratulated Jock but then he was embraced by his family and friends and I could see the happiness etched all over their faces. I then looked around at all of the other lads with their loved ones, and it struck me that no one had come to watch me. At that moment I felt a surge of sadness; I was in the middle of a group of people who were celebrating and it was obvious that they were happy and enjoying themselves. But I felt that there was a huge whole in the middle of me, and something was missing, and I felt completely lost.

I said my goodbyes to Jock. I was to be stationed at another base, and that was the last time I was to see him. Before I knew it I was on a train bound for RAF Hereford do continue with my training. I was to train to become a steward, as this was the profession I had chosen.

My decision to train as a Steward was completely opportunistic. I was in the recruitment centre and the recruiter said that the RAF needed stewards, and I thought "Why not!" I really did not know what it entailed, but all that I really wanted was to escape from home. When the training began I was intrigued to learn that I would be taught silver service waiting and the basics of catering, which involved everything other than the cooking. This type of training gave us the knowledge to prepare us to be stewards; I never at this time thought about, or had any expectations of anything beyond passing steward training.

At the beginning we had to learn how to set tables for functions. At times this could involve setting up for seven different courses. I found this fascinating, as I was lucky to get one course at home and now people were going to sit down and have seven. I remember that there was always plenty of food cooked; so much that at the end of service we could go into the kitchen and have a meal ourselves. I was even permitted to eat the best caviar, which I can tell you tastes horrible. I don't know what all the fuss is about.

I was there for thirteen weeks. The routine was very similar to what I had become used to, but with less emphasis on drill (which I was grateful for.) I was spending more time in a kitchen and dining room environment. It was here that I had my first brush with the Military Police. I was standing next to a chocolate vending machine, and someone had pointed out that if you pressed any button a bar of chocolate would be dispensed free of charge. Naturally I helped myself, but unfortunately a sergeant walked in and caught several of us. We were told to stand in a row and asked whether we had taken any chocolate. The guy next to me admitted that he had taken a bite of a bar that someone else had given him, but that as soon as he'd found out it had been stolen he threw it in the bin. I nearly burst out laughing at his unlikely story. We were all amazed to witness the sergeant reach into the bin and pull out what was left of the chocolate bar! I was marched in front of the group captain and given a warning, along with a £200 fine. That was the most expensive Mars Bar ever purchased.

After my stretch of training in Hereford I was stationed at RAF Honington, which would become my permanent base. I was to work in the officers' mess, which was not too bad. In the RAF the eating facilities are separate; the officers eat in the officers' mess, the sergeants in the sergeants mess and the airmen in the airmen's mess. The officers were always very pleasant to me, and in return I did everything to the best of my ability. Everything was going along just fine, until I got paid.

I decided to head into the local town, and it was during this visit that I spotted a bookmakers. At first I was apprehensive, but all it took was a welcoming man behind the counter to introduce me to the ins and outs of gambling. You could cut the atmosphere with a knife. As I looked around me I could see men huddled over newspapers looking to see if they could pick a winner from the day's racing. Some were puffing away on cigarettes, and the smoke filled the shop, the haze causing coughing fits among the customers (myself included.) This seemed to add to the drama and excitement in a strange sort of way. As I took my seat I glanced up and caught the eye of the man opposite me. He had that weathered look of someone who has been through a few campaigns; a thousand lines had been engraved onto his face. He quickly returned his gaze back to the paper. The entire day's racing was being broadcast through one speaker which was positioned in the corner of the shop. The next race was about to start, so I placed a bet with the others at the counter. "Good luck," came the response from the cashier, and then the race was off. The excitement at times seemed unbearable, as the commentator relayed what was happening. The horses were neck and neck - nothing between them - each horse seemed to be responding to the jockey's urging and there was nothing separating them as they jumped the last fence. All around me the punters were shouting for their own horse and then suddenly the winner was announced and newspapers would be flung into the air and a few choice words were shouted. As I caught the eye of the man opposite again it seemed as though another line had appeared on his face. He might have seen one appear on mine also. My horse had lost.

This brought back the excitement of betting my pocket money on the horses with my father, and I began craving the thrill. And sometimes...

(Rarely...)

I won.

It was fun and I began to become immersed in it.

In no time at all I was betting on two or three horses in one race. At every opportunity I would hop on the bus and go and gamble my wages away. I would usually find that it had all gone about half way through the month, so when the other lads were going out I had to make excuses and stay in.

One night, while they were out, an opportunity presented itself to me. I noticed a wallet by one of the beds, and almost without hesitation I took it, emptied it of its contents and threw it away. The urge to gamble was greater than the fear of being caught, so I wasn't too bothered about the commotion from the man who had lost his wallet. No one ever knew, so I repeated the act many times over the following six months or so. Then, one day, the game was up. The Military Police arrested me for the thefts. I tried the usual lines: "I don't know what you're talking about," and "You have the wrong person!" But they had my fingerprints on one of the wallets, and there was no talking my way out of that one. I was placed in front of the group captain and swiftly sentenced to a 49 day imprisonment.

I served this sentence on the camp, being confined to the guard house. I think the reason I was kept here was just that

I would be humiliated. Each day I would be marched up and down the camp to get my meals, in full view of anyone who chose to watch. At first this was embarrassing, but I got used to it. The rest of my time was spent either cleaning the guardhouse or on drill. At the end of my 49 days I was in front of my squadron leader (who was head of catering) who said simply "I hope you have learnt your lesson." An abrupt end to a difficult time.

I was back to work immediately as if nothing had happened at all. I soon got back into the daily routine, but I found that imprisonment had not erased the thoughts of gambling that now occupied my mind. Within a few months of being released I found myself back in the betting shop, gambling all my wages away. Addiction can be an incredibly lonely place. Gambling had looked fun from the outside, but I now felt like I was living a nightmare. Before long I was stealing again, and within about three months I was facing a military court marshall. This time the punishment was greater: six months in Colchester Military Corrective Training Centre and dismissal from the RAF.

Two military policemen collected me. Very little conversation took place on the journey but what I do remember is that they said that I was to expect hell in Colchester. As the minibus pulled up outside Colchester and the doors were opened I was made to run at the double with a Sergeant's voice right by my ear bellowing orders at me. "Don't look at me! Stand straight! Don't talk until I say so! I am to be referred to as Sergeant!" I made a mistake at this point and said "Yes sir." He went berserk. In my mind I was doing exactly what he was ordering me to do, but wisely I kept that to myself.

I was then strip searched and given clothing to wear, although this time I was issued with boiler suit. This was partly because I was not in the military anymore, but also because if ever a piece of clothing was invented to crush spirits, it was the boiler suit. I was then escorted at the double to my sleeping quarters, which were exactly like those in basic training. The billet had a wooden interior with a stove in the middle which kept it heated. The left and right walls of the room each had ten beds lined up along them, each with a mattress and blankets. There were no washing facilities; these were elsewhere. I put what little I had on the bed that was assigned to me and immediately joined a group outside that was doing drill. I didn't get a chance to introduce myself as talking on the parade ground was not permitted. Failure to comply was strictly enforced by a punch in the ribs, which usually did the trick.

After the drill was finished we were marched at the double back into our billets to prepare them and ourselves for inspection. It was during this time that I was able to introduce myself, and I found out that some people were being discharged, while others were just there for a few weeks or months before returning to their bases. Then the remainder of the day was dedicated to fitness, particularly route marches with kit bags on our backs. At the beginning it was extremely hard, and I certainly was not as fit as I should have been. I often had to stop and throw up, much to the annoyance of the rest of the group. They would be marching double time on the spot whilst I recovered enough to resume the march. Eventually, as new inmates arrived I became one of the fitter, more experienced of the group, so I was the one marching double time while they vomited.

I didn't make any friends, but I think it's rare that people do in these establishments. Nevertheless we did learn as a group to look after each other, often helping when someone was struggling with fitness, or sharing duties.

When the lights went out at night we were so exhausted that before we knew it the sergeant would be in barking orders for us to get up. This was the set routine that passed by week by week and month by month.

Sometimes I can still feel the freezing cold conditions during that winter. Often the billet was not heated as it should be. Some nights I could see my own breath, even in the darkness. I would often shuffle my feet and clasp my hands in a vain effort to try and keep warm. When the door to the billet was opened a cold wind would come in, often accompanied by snow.

The time that I spent in Colchester was extremely hard. It pushed me to the very limits, sometimes even to complete exhaustion. But I got through it, and when it was time for me to be released I was the fittest that I had ever been.

When I was discharged I was concerned by one nagging question: what was I going to do now?

Escape to Greece and Corfu

I travelled to Scotland to see if I could stay with my mum. By now she was living with another man in his house, but I thought I'd give it a go. As I knocked on the front door he answered it and immediately told me I wasn't welcome and closed the door in my face. What could I do? It was a long shot but I decided to go to the police station. I knew that they certainly did have accommodation, but would they let me stay in a cell overnight? Even if they did, is that really what I wanted?

As I entered the station the hairs on the back of my neck stood up. Surely the only time to come here was in handcuffs, and here I was walking in of my own accord. I hastily brushed aside my initial pangs of fear, and as I approached the desk sergeant I nervously said "I need a bed for the night." He looked me up and down and a wry smile crossed his face. "Really?" he muttered, "and what makes you think that we are a hotel?" I explained the situation that I was in: that I had no money and no home. He must have taken pity on me because he decided to dispatch a police car with two officers in it. I was invited to sit in the back, and off we went. They stopped the car, got out and went up the path and towards the front door of the house that my mother and sister were living in. I watched as the door opened and the officers went inside. They were in there for what felt like days. In reality I think that it was only about a half an hour. As I looked at the house I could make out the figure of a little girl: it was my sister Margaret. And then suddenly the front door opened once more, the officers walked back up the path, got back into the car, turned around to me and said "You have no chance. They are not going to let you stay under any circumstance." With that I took a deep breath and slumped into the seat. As the car pulled away from the house I looked up and in the bedroom window I saw my sister waving with tears running down her face.

We all returned to the police station and the officers relayed to the desk sergeant what had happened. After a few moments he said he was sorry, that I couldn't stay there and that I would have to leave the Police Station. Unless I committed an offence I could not stay in the cells. So on to the streets I was sent, with very little money and nowhere to live. It was whilst I was roaming the streets in the wind and freezing cold conditions that a thought crossed my mind: "Why don't I pick up a brick and throw it through a shop window?" With that one simple action all my problems would be solved. I would be in a warm environment, with food in my stomach and a roof over my head. So I picked up a brick, but something strange happened. I couldn't muster up the courage to throw it through the window. I stayed in the area for a few days sleeping on benches. At night the conditions were almost unbearable, with the temperature dropping fast. I would often wake up in the night shivering, curl into a ball and hope that would help. Obviously there were the risks. I was all too aware that there were plenty of people ready to take advantage of, or attack someone like me. I was lucky that I never had to face that type of situation, but the threat was bad enough. I decided that there was nothing left for me to do other than hitch a lift to Sunderland, thinking that maybe I could stay with some relations. I managed to reach Sunderland but with nowhere to live what could I do? I then noticed that there was a Salvation Army hostel so I stayed there for a night. I arrived at the hostel late at night, and they welcomed me in and offered me a cup of tea. Because it was so late I was given some blankets and shown to a bed for the night. As I entered the room I could make out the form of a body in another bed, and I could hear him snoring away. The smell was unbelievable, like a hundred pairs of unwashed socks soaked in melted blue cheese. I quickly made my bed in the pitch black, and as I got under the covers I tried to comfort myself with the thought at least I had a roof over my head. A whiff of the room hit me like a wall of human waste, so I quickly put my head under the covers and drifted off to sleep. I was awoken by a knock on the door and a voice saying breakfast was being served, and I needed no further prompting. I was out of the bed down the stairs and before long I was tucking into a full English breakfast with four slices of toast and a mug of hot coffee and with that I was ready to look for my family. I made a few inquiries with the hostel staff but no one could give me any information that was helpful to me. So I thanked the Salvation Army staff and left the hostel to search different parts of Sunderland. But I couldn't find anyone so I gave up on the North East and hitched another ride to London.

I found myself in Kingston-upon-Thames, and by chance I saw an advertisement for a chamber person in a local hotel so I applied for the job. What's more, it provided accommodation. I got it, and now I was making beds in hotel rooms. After a while I began to feel claustrophobic and restless, and once again I found myself drawn to the betting shop. Gambling seemed to offer an alternative to the daily routine of work, and the excitement and thrill of placing a bet became a compulsion. I now had to do it. I often left the bookmakers having lost all of my wages. A deep depression would set in and I would often spend hour after hour alone and penniless in my room

Then one day as I was cleaning one of the rooms I saw two chequebooks, and without thinking I stole them, packed my bags and hastily left. I then went to a post office and gave some story about my needing to get to Greece as my gran was dying, and they believed me. This is how I managed to convince the Post Office staff that I needed a temporary three month passport. I found a photograph of myself and then I said that the only identification that I had was my chequebook, that I was not from this part of the country and that I had received an emergency call saying that I needed to get to Greece immediately. Of course the chequebook was in the name of the person I had stolen it from, but combined with my story and a few tears the staff believed me, and with their comforting words ringing in my ears I was issued a temporary three month passport, and I bought a bus ticket from Victoria bus station to Athens. The journey took three days.

The journey itself was fairly uneventful. We set off from Victoria and then got a ferry across to France and made our way through Europe. I remember looking up out of the bus window and seeing a beautiful chalet precariously perched on a cliff edge with snow surrounding its perimeter. The heat in the bus was unbearable and we made frequent stops for toilets and food. On one of these stops I found that I needed cash so when we stopped I found a Bureau de Change. It was so easy for me to cash a cheque; I simply made out the cheque for a hundred French Francs, smiled at the cashier, and they handed over the money. I also cashed another cheque in Thessalonica in Greece for a Hundred Drachma. All of the transactions went through smoothly and I always walked away with the cash. I still felt nervous every time; there was a lot at stake, especially because I was stranded in another country if it went wrong.

I arrived in Athens hot and tired. I did what most tourists did. I visited the sights; the Acropolis, for instance. It didn't seem to be too far up the hill, but as I started upwards I passed tourists making the return journey, who seemed hot and flustered. About a quarter of the way up I too was feeling the heat, and I had to stop and buy an ice cold bottle of water from a vendor. When I eventually reached the top I really was not all that impressed; it just looked like an old ruin missing a lot of its original features. Just as I was consoling myself with the knowledge that it would be far easier to get back down again, a man approached me and said "Picture sir, I can take your picture next to the Acropolis for 10 Drachma. For a brief moment I was tempted but then I realised that it would probably not be a good idea; thoughts of the photo making its way to the police flashed across my mind. I thanked the man and said "No photo." I knew by now that the police would know of the stolen cheque books and it would only be a matter of time before I was caught. But for now my mind was set on enjoying the holiday and getting back down the hill. I looked around Athens to see if there was a bookmakers but I could not find one.

It was at St Agma Square in Athens where I would come to cash cheques when I was getting short of money. On one particularly hot day I was walking along, and as I looked to my left there was a set of steps leading down into what looked like a café or perhaps a bar. Out of nowhere someone took a hold of my arm, not too forcefully, and took me downwards. I was intrigued and curious, so I let him guide me as we entered what initially looked like an ordinary room. Once my eyes became accustomed to the dimly lit surroundings I realised that this was a bar. He motioned for me to sit down on a bar stool and he then offered me a free glass of Champagne on the house which I gulped back. "Great!" I thought, "I like this," and he promptly offered me a bottle. I was beginning to feel slightly drunk, and with each sip (gulp) of Champagne my thoughts were "I could get used to this." With every passing moment my worries disintegrated, melting away in a drunken haze. Eventually the free Champagne ran out, and the barman said I would have to pay for more if I wanted it. I informed him that unfortunately I had no cash on me but I did have my chequebook. He smiled and said "That's no problem, sir." That was sweet music to my ears and after I had used two cheques and had drunk nearly two bottles, two beautiful women came up to me, one on either side. I don't remember much about them, other than that one had blonde hair and the other brunette, and that I thought they were really good looking. They were certainly making me feel most welcome, and with a hand from each of them on my thighs I was getting hot under the collar. I was quiet happy to play along and share my Champagne with them. As they were whispering sweet nothings in my ear, they managed to get me to part with another couple of cheques and another two bottles. I was getting rather drunk by now and the barman said he could not accept any more cheques. I thought that was fair enough, so I looked around for my two companions, and as silently as they appeared they had disappeared. I had a smile on my face as I left.

As I climbed off my bar stool and made my way up the steps back into the square I noticed that by now it was dark, but I chuckled to myself - I almost burst out laughing - what would they think or say when the cheques were returned to the bar unpaid by the bank? I would have liked to have seen the expressions on their faces then.

After spending a week in Athens I became bored and decided to fly to Corfu. It was a beautiful island and within hours had made myself at home. I had booked myself into a local hotel. The price was not too bad and the view from my window was stunning. As I looked out I could see the waves of the ocean, and the horizon was strewn with boats of every type; passenger liners; speed boats; boats that take tourists around the island, and the beach was full of sun bathers. As I closed my window I decided to go out and investigate. I remember walking down a long winding road that led down to the beach, and the road was lined with trees on both sides. As I reached the bottom and stood on the beach I looked around me, and would you believe it? I had stumbled onto a nudist beach. The dilemma was as follows: Do I go and strip off and join the party, or do I walk along trying to look as though I am not familiar with the surroundings and that it is okay to remain clothed. I chose the latter option. It was an embarrassing but worthwhile experience.

The days went by relatively quickly and each was much like the previous. Often I would go for a walk past the vineyards and I just used to reach over from the side of the road and grab a bunch of grapes. They were sweet and delicious, and they quenched my thirst from the hot midday sun. I found the islanders warm and accommodating, and quick to engage in conversation, but usually I would be guarded as I certainly did not want to let slip my identity or activities. After any consumption of alcohol there was the risk of saying something that I would regret so I was always very careful. That said, I had hired a moped and was eating at expensive restaurants; often the very best that the island had to offer. Being an island in the Mediterranean there was always a choice of fresh fish caught that day, and I would have a beer to wash it down. And all the while the cheques were running out.

I walked around the island for a few days savouring the sights and sounds, but before long I had used up all the cheques and I had to leave the hotel. I decided I would go to the beach and sleep, but I would go when it was dark. As I sat on the sand looking out on to the sea and up to the stars I knew that the adventure was about to end, but I did not let this thought remain for long. As I curled into a ball with a blanket for warmth I drifted off to sleep. A pack of growling, sniffing dogs were the next thing I sensed. They had me surrounded. I slowly stood up and the dogs' growls turned into barks. In my best manly voice I said "There's a good doggy go away leave me alone." The pack advanced. I had probably given them an open invitation to have me for dinner. There was only one thing for it: I grabbed the nearest stick and a few stones and I lashed out at them. This seemed to do the trick and they retreated. I then made my way off the beach and back onto the main road, and as I looked around one solitary dog was still following me. With one more throw of a stone the dog got the message and slunk off.

It was over, and I only had one place left to go: The British Consul.

I went to their offices and made up some story about having no money to get home. They asked me my name, which presented a dilemma. Did I give them my real name, or the one on my passport and chequebook? I knew the game was up; after all I had left a paper trail across Europe. I came clean and told them, and that same day I was taken from the consul by two Greek Police Officers, put into a police car and driven across Corfu to the court. I was totally confused as to what was happening, as neither the police officers nor the judge spoke English. I was taken up a stairwell, and on either side people were crying. As I stood in front of the judge there was a conversation going on which I could not understand but a lawyer interpreted that the judge said that the British consul would pay for my ticket home and I would be deported. I felt a sense of relief, despite my awareness that I would be in trouble when I got back to Britain. At least I would be in prison somewhere that I could speak the language.

From there I was driven to the British consul who issued me with a one way ticket home. That very same day I found myself on a boat from Corfu to Brindisi which is on the tip of Italy. I was on my way back home, and I suspected what awaited me on my arrival. As we sailed into Dover I recognised them standing just the other side of passport control. The two C.I.D Officers looked at me and said "Ian Bartlett you are under arrest."

Borstal & Oxford University

I appeared in front of Inner London Crown Court and I was given a six month borstal sentence. This type of punishment was very similar to my time in Military Prison. It was intended as a short, sharp shock in the hope that it would deter young men from reoffending. Unfortunately it was more of a breeding ground that would give rise to more and more serious crimes. I was not new to this environment, so it was not such a shock as it otherwise might have been.

After a few days I was assigned a job sewing mail bags in a building within the prison walls. This was a tedious job and boredom often set in. On these occasions my mind tended to drift away. Usually I would end up on some exotic island enjoying the sun and the scenery, cocktail in hand and not a care in the world. I would be brought slamming down to earth with a slap across the ear from a prison officer with a shout of "Wake up! Stop day dreaming or you won't get your wages this week!" That would bring me out of dreamland and back to the sewing.

Our wages were minimal; each week they paid for essentials such as toiletries, and if there was anything left over it might just about stretch to pay for sweets or tobacco. On pay day I used to make myself physically sick by eating too many Mars Bars. They couldn't be left in the cell, because if I so much as went for a shower they would have been gone. Some other inmates would watch for opportunities to steal, but if they got caught they would be severely beaten up. The saying is true: There is no honour among thieves.

I played in goal for the borstal football team. Visiting teams used to come in to the prison to play against us and we were in the local league but unfortunately we never had any away games. I must have caught the eye of the coaches as I was picked to play for the league side against another county. This gave me permission to go out of the prison for a day. So, one Sunday I was escorted out by a prison officer and I played in a 5-1 defeat. I have an excuse, of course: I did not know my defence so the communication was pretty sketchy to say the least. Nevertheless it was an enjoyable day out and as a consolation, and despite the setback we actually went on to win the league that season. We all became extremely fit, and with no vices like alcohol or drugs to distract us most of our time was spent in the gym or running around the field inside the borstal.

I never thought about my future or where I was heading; I was young and I was going to live from day to day. I never had any type of experience that would help me to decide what to do with my life. I never had a role model who would have been able to guide and advise me. In the absence of a strong parental role model I was destined to drift with no ambition. I sensed that I was becoming hardened to what the world had to offer, and for me that did not seem to be much, other than the expectation that gambling and crime and further prison sentences were inevitable.

When I was in locked in my cell at night there would regularly be a bang on the wall with a shout of "Have you got any sugar mate?"

"No" I always replied. A few seconds would pass and then,

"Have you got any tea mate?"

"No!" again.

"How about tobacco then?

"No."

Then the guy next door would threaten to smash my face in, and I wouldn't believe him. Still, I was awake most of the night wondering how I would defend myself against this idiot. For all I knew he could quiet easily have made an implement out of razor blades to stab me, or put a big battery into a sock to use as a sling. This was all crazy of course, but night time is night time.

I heard the footsteps of a prison officer approach. He opened my cell and I made my way to the washroom, all the time looking behind me just waiting for this guy. Sure enough he was right behind me, and as I entered the washroom I made sure I took a sink next to the wall so at least I would have an opportunity to see him coming. He looked at me and said "Alright mate?" I said "Yes." Then he then continued to have his wash and said absolutely nothing to me about the night before. There are many instances when people do get stabbed over the most petty of things, but also there are times when people are weighing you up to see if you are an easy target. I always stood my ground. The consequences of not doing so are not worth considering.

I remember sitting in the TV room watching the news, and seeing warships. They were heading for the Falklands. As I looked across the room I saw one of the prison officers wipe away a tear from his eye. I thought he must have been in the forces earlier in his life. This was the start of the Falklands War. In my head even this provided a potential escape; perhaps there would be an amnesty for prisoners and I would be able to go to war. But that opportunity never arose, and the rest of my sentence passed without much event.

I came out of borstal and headed for Oxford. I rented a small room in the city, but within a short period of time history was repeating itself; I was gambling and I was running out of money. I don't know how anyone ex-prisoner can lead an honest and productive life when the set of circumstances we find ourselves in are exactly the same when we come out as when we first went in. It seemed that it was a vicious circle with no opportunity for change.

Necessity always leads to resourcefulness, and it was at this point that I discovered a new way of making money quickly. I would just walk into the Porter's Lodges in the University Colleges and help myself to the mail which had been placed in pigeon holes. Cheque books were easy to find amongst the other assorted post. I could quiet easily take two cheque books in a day, with each cheque book holding thirty-five cheques. As long as I stayed under £50 when I cashed the cheque no questions were asked concerning identification, so I used to write cheques out for £45. One chequebook would therefore provide me with an easy £1575, which would always, without fail, go straight on gambling. In one day I could get £720 just by walking from one cashier to another eight times in the morning and eight times in the afternoon. As quickly as the cheques ran out, I acquired more.

There were a few times when I thought that the cashiers were suspicious of me and on one of these occasions the woman behind the counter was taking just too long to serve me. Something felt wrong. She was asking me suspicious questions that she had no need to ask about: whether I was on holiday, and "Had I been in there before?" This was like a flashing red warning light, so when I saw her right hand reaching down below the counter as if she was going to press an alarm bell, I immediately turned around and left the bank. I mingled in with the students and tourists expertly and I was lost in the crowd, but even when this type of incident occurred I would give it a few hours and go to another bank to resume cashing cheques. Just like during my earlier thefts in prison, the impulse to gamble overrode the consequences of being caught. This type of crime is faceless; you really don't appreciate the harm it might cause. Knowing this, in the brief moments I did reflect I convinced myself that I was hurting no one except maybe the bank, and clearly they could afford it.

The problem was that I left a paper trail. The knock on the door from the police was only a matter of time; they had camera, fingerprint and hand writing evidence. Sure enough the knock came, and I took the usual the "No comment" route when I was interviewed by the police. This really was pointless as they had all of the evidence they needed to convict me. I was in front of a judge again, this time at Oxford Crown Court. Two and a half years. The sentence lengths were creeping up.

The cells at the police station were small. I had a tiny mattress and a toilet which was monitored by camera. In these cells all privacy, and with it all dignity, is denied. The food is not great; I would usually refuse it and wait until I was bailed out or transferred to prison. The smells could be horrendous; often the previous resident had not used the toilet and might possibly have been sick all over the place, and to top that you might have to share a cell with a drunk or someone coming down from heroin. You have to be on your toes, as at any moment an argument might start and you could be called upon to fight. There is a small buzzer on the inside of the cell door in case of emergency, but more often than not the police officer would ignore it or fail to hear it. And constantly throughout the day and night you would get people banging on the cell doors. Some would have serious mental health issues, while others would just do it to wind up the custody staff. I would always find that if you treated the custody staff with courtesy they would treat you in the same way.

I knew what to expect as I had now been to a few of Her Majesty's Prisons. The routine is always the same, although around this time the conditions were far worse than they are today. While the toilet facilities in the police cells were appalling, in prison cells they were non-existent. If I wanted to go to the toilet in the night I would use a pot, and that would be done in full view of two other men. In the cells, dignity goes right out of the window. When the wing is opened up in the morning everyone takes their pot to empty it down the toilet. I have seen many a fight involving spilt pots. There were also no TVs like there are today. The conditions overall were far worse. You have to remember these were old Victorian prisons.

One thing I learnt whilst I was in prison is that I could not afford to show any weakness. If I ever had, there were many who ready to capitalise. The weak become prey in prison. It is amazing how people can condition themselves to deal with whatever is thrown at them. I got my head down and worked, at first cleaning the wing then after about six months I got a job in the kitchen. In a prison this is seen as the job to have; the benefits are obvious - you are out of your cell during the day and you get to eat lots of food. After a while I managed to get a job on the prison farm which was located outside of the prison. I was transferred to live in a billet which was in the prison grounds, and it was absolutely freezing. We used to be woken at 6am - an hour earlier than the rest of the prison, and then we were taken to the farm. You might think that sounds like a great job, but unfortunately for us we had a civilian watching our work. He used to get us picking up stones in a field and building a massive pile. The field would take about a week to clear, and at the end of that week he would order us to move them to the other end. I would have associated this kind of 'work' with an American chain gang, but this is what we had to do. I did not last long doing this and as soon as possible I was back on the wing in the main prison.

Each day was almost identical, unless a fight erupted and we are all banged up until everything was back under control. At regular intervals the cells would be searched for drugs and contraband. It was at this time that scaffolding was erected on the outside of the prison and unknown to me two inmates on the top landing of the wing had made a whole in the roof of their cell. This must have taken a lot of time, and each day they had covered it up. One morning there was great commotion and we were kept in our cells. They had escaped and were on the run! Of course when anyone hears of an escape all of the cell doors are banged by the inmates in celebration. The joy was short-lived; they were captured and brought back within hours.

Whilst in prison you do make friendships but these are rarely followed through, and friendships are rarely kept once you are released. You have to remember that when you go into prison you know no one. You don't know what crime anyone has committed and you certainly don't know what they are capable of so it's best not to give away too much information that might be useful to a malicious inmate.

I was nervous a whole week before my parole hearing and I could not sleep. I was of course hoping that my parole hearing would be successful so I would be released early. In prison there is excitement when people go up for a parole. If they are granted parole it usually means that they will be released a month later. However it could go the other way, and if parole is denied, it can be another five years before they are eligible to appeal again. One mid-afternoon I was finally called before the parole board. I entered a small room, and as I looked ahead I saw three men dressed in suits who told me to take a seat. Then they commenced to ask me a series of questions, some relating to my offences and others to the steps I had taken to rehabilitate myself. In other words they were looking to see whether I was remorseful, and how likely it was that I would reoffend. These questions lasted around ten minutes and when they had finished they informed me that they would let me know their decision in due course. I got up and left the room to return to my cell.

Some parole decisions can take up to an agonising six months. I had to wait for three months. Then one day as I was on the landing in the wing I was summoned to the wing office and I was handed a letter informing me I had not been given parole. I decided that I would keep my head down and get on with the rest of my sentence. There is always a great expectation and excitement when you are nearing your release date, and the last two months of my sentence seemed to take forever to complete. On my last night, as was the custom, I gave everything away to the friends I had made. Prisoners always promised that they would send in some money or visit their friends, but the best laid plans go out of the window when those prison gates are opened.

After serving two years of my sentence I found myself yet again at the prison gates with £40 in my pocket. I had been released, and as I left a voice followed me out into the unforgiving world I was to step back into. "See you again soon..." it taunted.

The sentences were increasing each time; first forty-nine days, then two lots of six months, then two and a half years. There was only one way this was going. For me prison had become an occupational hazard. I still had to feed my gambling addiction, which just would not go away. A cocktail of gambling, crime, alcohol and eventually cocaine would define my life during these years.

Back to Work

Between prison sentences I managed to find some work as a kitchen porter in a nursing home. This position offered me a chance to do something positive. Without work, thoughts of gambling would have crept into my mind, and they would have quickly taken over. The job itself involved working in the kitchen washing pots and pans, but as time passed by I was given more responsibility and I ended up cooking for the residents and staff. The opportunity came by chance; the cook was off sick one day and the matron asked if I could do it. I must have done a good job because I was soon asked to do it full time. I worked there for six months and they gave me a reference so I could move forward into other jobs. After a while I managed to get a job working for Oxford City Council at the Town Hall as a keeper. In that job I got to meet people like Ted Heath and Stephen Hawking. Unfortunately I was on holiday when Nelson Mandela was given freedom of the city. I helped set up boxing events, staging for orchestras and student fayres. In the Town Hall there is a room which holds some treasures that have been given to the city over the years. Twice a year this room was opened to the public, and I attended these events. I was also occasionally on locking up and alarming duty, so I got to know the different Lord Mayors and the councillors for the city. As part of a team that was ultimately responsible for the smooth running of the Town Hall I engaged with lots of different people, some of whom became friends, but even at this point I was gambling my wages away most months.

I then found myself in a relationship. I had met Rose in a nightclub and we hit it off straight away. I must admit I was a bit tipsy but I must have made an impression because within three months I had moved into her three bedroom house. It had a garden at the front and back, and we would often have barbeques in the back garden, inviting neighbours and friends over. For once everything seemed to be fine.

We had holidays in New York, and one time we visited Rose's sister in Queens. During our two week stay we managed to visit the Statue of Liberty (although we didn't brave the queues to go up.) On another night we travelled up the Hudson River admiring the view. I remember looking over and seeing women dancing to the music coming from a DJ, and these women were so loud that you could hear everything they were saying from fifty feet away. Apparently 'loud' is an important part of how to communicate in New York, and I have never seen so many diamonds and so much gold draped on women as I did that night. I also had the opportunity to go to the Bronx which was a bit surreal as I was the only white man. This was not something I was used to. We visited another of Rose's sisters who lived there and when we went to McDonalds. You should have seen the kids' expressions as I walked in. You would have thought that they had seen a ghost, such was the scarcity of white faces in the area.

I really enjoyed my trips to New York; we always went when it was hot and I like the heat. I remember as a child watching some TV programme where you see a fire hydrant which has been opened with children dancing by it being soaked by the water. And when you looked ahead you could see a train line overhead. Well if you can imagine that, it really was exactly that image that I saw when I visited the Bronx. On another Holiday we went to Jamaica and visited Rose's other sister and mother. I remember landing in Kingston and as I looked around me I was the only white man getting off. For a brief moment I thought I had heard the announcement wrong and I was about to sit down again when Rose said that the white people were staying on the plane to go to Montego Bay, and with that I got off the plane. We stayed at Rose's sister's in constant spring; the accommodation was fine and we had someone around the house who was called the "helper" (basically the woman did everything - cooking, cleaning - you name it she did it.)

I bonded with Rose's brother in law, who reliably informed me that he was an ex-policeman, and I had no reason to doubt him. He was a big, stocky man with a huge beard. You would not want to get on the wrong side of him, and it was on a night out to a local restaurant that he lifted up the back of his shirt and showed me a sub-machine gun. I was astonished. We travelled to the restaurant and the scenery and the food was excellent. The table was on the end of a pontoon and the view was of the sun going down looking over the sea and the stars flickering brightly. At one point I started to get a little concerned as the waiter was adamant about something which I could not make out as the conversation was in Patois, which is nearly impossible to interpret unless you are a local. Anyhow, a thought crossed my mind as their conversation heated up. If only the waiter had known about the sub-machine gun he might be a little less enthusiastic about putting his point across. As it was, the evening ended with no further incident.

During that holiday we all spent the day down on the beach and we were treated to a meal in a wooden hut. We ate curried goat, sword fish, plantain and an array of Jamaican specialities. The food was astonishing and the flavours were incredible. After we finished our meal we lay on the beach soaking up the sun and out of the corner of my eye I saw a Rastafarian man coming up the beach and it looked like he had a basket in his hand. As he got closer he approached me and said "Ya want a massage English man?" and I declined, but thanked him for asking. I suppose this was a way to make a living; Jamaica has abject poverty which runs alongside opulence. That's the way it is.

But throughout even this relatively happy time I was still gambling, and this hung like a cloud. I continued to work at the Town Hall for three years, and then I moved on to work for the County Council. Then an opportunity came up to work for Oxford University looking after 120 international students and two houses. This meant that I moved out of the house with my girlfriend and into a flat that came with the job.

It was at this time that a two year relationship with cocaine began. I was introduced to it by a so called friend who said that it would make me talk a lot and give me an ability to drink for England without getting drunk. Like a fool I was taken in and so one night I snorted a line and indeed it did do as he had said and I was really enjoying it. Then my friend said that he had a lump of cocaine and could I hold it for him? He sweetened the deal by saying I could help myself at no financial cost so I did. With no limits on the amount I could have I started to take more and more and this began to affect my work as I was up all night taking coke, so I ended up taking it first thing in the morning to keep me awake. This cycle continued from month to month and with that I was being asked to hold more and more. When I did manage to sleep I would wake up with my nose completely blocked and I would often have to blow my nose. When I was in the company of other people I would be constantly sniffing and wiping my nose. I watched as the dealers chopped up the cocaine and mixed it with another powder (aspirin at best) but I was assured that I would not get the cut stuff. They weighed it out in grams and placed it in wraps which they were selling for £50 a time. This was a profitable business for those who were involved. As the months rolled into one another the drug itself took an unexpected turn. It caused me to want to cut myself off from the real world and be by myself. I would often pace up and down my flat and I started to watch videos which were not good for me. And then my so called friend said that I had to pay for the drug now, which meant that I would have to find the cash. This drug had promised fun but in reality over time it became a living nightmare.

My relationship with Rose had deteriorated considerably, to the point where I was no longer contacting her. The cocaine was sucking the very life out of me. I would end up taking it to help me through the working days. I would take some before and after, so it framed my working life. Interwoven with gambling and drinking, more crime was inevitable, and soon I was stealing again. It must have looked as though I had a normal, comfortable life with a job and home, but my multiple addictions needed fuelling with more money. It must have been a confusing time for Rose when my temperament started to change. As the drug took its toll I became very snappy at anything and I took it out on her by failing to call her or meet her when we had arranged a time. I had become totally unreliable and self-centred.

I started sneaking into corridors in the colleges, knocking and doors and emptying the vacated flats of cash. In my relentless pursuit of money I did this time and time again. Only recently have I reflected on the terror I must have brought to that community. Although apologies can't fix anything, they are a start, and I am certainly sorry. At the time I felt no remorse; in fact my ability to cover my tracks expertly was making me feel invincible. It was by chance that when the knock finally came the drugs had disappeared with the owner. I was sitting in my office working when two police officers appeared. I was shocked and relieved at the arrest.

I was taken to the police station and questioned for 72 hours but I was not coming easy; they would have to work for it if they were going to convict me. I stuck to the "No comment" answers to all of the questions that were asked of me, and at the end of the 72 hours I appeared before the Magistrate's Court, my solicitor applied for bail and bail was granted with conditions attached. The conditions were that I was not to enter any university college, I was to relinquish all of the keys that I held for the properties that I looked after, and that I was to sign on at the police station every day at 2pm.

The police officers used harassment as a tactic, often knocking on my door in the early hours just to 'inquire how

I was.' I replied with a sarcastic "How are you, officer?" At least that showed I wasn't intimidated. I was short of money so I started stealing again. I entered a college building and I realised that a group was going to be staying. As I watched out of one of the windows a bus turned up at one of the gates and people got off and went into the porters lodge. While they were being issued their room keys, I hid in one of the shower rooms on the landing. I could hear voices, so I waited until I heard someone say that the group had to go to a welcome reception in ten minutes, then I heard people leave the building and close the entrance door. I then came out of the shower and looked to see people going from the other buildings across the courtyard. At that I went to the third landing and knocked on the door. No one answered so I turned the handle and to my bewilderment the door had been left open. I then entered the room and on one of the beds there was a handbag. I emptied the cash out of the purse and placed it back in the bag. I then looked up and I could see a key behind a glass panel. I took it from behind the panel and then I knocked on the door of the room opposite. Again, no one answered. I put the key in the lock and to my amazement the lock turned and I entered the room. I did exactly what I had done to the previous room. In fact I did this to twelve rooms in the building but on the top floor the fire escape doors connected with the next building and I moved from building to building. Sometimes there was nothing in the rooms and I would come out and lock the door as if no one had entered. I then heard voices as people were returning to their rooms and I then hastily made my exit out of the college. It was the very next day that I heard a loud bang on my front door of the flat and I knew that it was the police and that they had come to arrest me. I could think of no solution other than to run. I slid the window of the flat open and dropped 30 feet out of the window. Somehow my legs didn't break – I'll never know how – and I was now officially on the run.

On the Run

There was no way I could have stayed in Oxford. There might be police around any corner, so I needed a plan to evade being caught. Just as I was wondering how I could get away from the constant threat, a bus to Witney – a nearby Oxfordshire town – pulled up next to me. Without thinking any further, I jumped on board and purchased a ticket. Following this short journey I walked along the High Street, looking to see where I could stay. After a while I went into a coffee shop to mull over my options. I knew the most important thing would be to find a place to stay, so after finishing my coffee I looked at hotels. After a bit of research and exploring I found one I could afford and arranged a week-long stay.

That first night I was completely exhausted. I fell into bed and twelve hours later I regained consciousness. When I woke up I peered into my wallet and realised that I would, out of necessity, be going back into Oxford in search of money. And so after spending my last £40 in the bookmakers I returned. I was now more cautious than ever. I knew the colleges like the back of hand and if ever the police were to chase me I knew that my knowledge would come in handy.

I had my head down, scurrying along the pavement trying my utmost not to be noticed when I identified a potential target. I saw students going back and forth to classes in a building which was situated off the main road in a side street. As I tailgated them from one building to the next, someone held open a door for me and I politely said "Thank you." They must have mistaken me for a teacher.

As I entered the building my heart was racing but I kept calm and knew that if I was challenged I would have a convincing answer to get me out of a tight corner. On this occasion I was not stopped.

I went up a stairwell and as I got close to a secured door at the top, the door suddenly opened and a woman smiled at me and held the door open. I thanked her and went through the door, which then shut behind me. I noticed that it had a secure code entry system. "Perfect!" I thought. I would be able to hear if anyone was trying to get in so I could either hide or get out. As I looked around me I could see that this was an accommodation block for international students. I'd hit the jackpot! International students often kept currency in their rooms. After a while of waiting and listening I started to knock on doors to see if anyone was in, but to my relief the students had all gone out.

There was no answer at the first door so I pressed my shoulder against the lock. It didn't budge, so I moved onto the next door. I took a different approach this time, running at it with the full weight of my body. I bundled into the door, and this one gave way, bits of wood flying everywhere. I rifled through the draws and the wardrobe: nothing. Then I looked under the bed and there was a suitcase with a padlock on it. As I snapped the lock off my eyes immediately came to rest on a money belt and as I opened the zip I could see that it was full of foreign currency. I grabbed the money belt and put it around my waist, leaving the premises the way I had entered. I quickly hailed a taxi back to Witney. I paid the driver with a £50 note which I had managed to extract from the money belt without him even noticing. I then went straight back to the hotel and locked myself in my room. The sweat was pouring off me, when I saw the contents; there was over £1800 in English money and an additionally £1200 in Russian Roubles. I was gobsmacked: what a result!

At first I did not know the value of the Russian money and I was going to throw it away as I thought it would be near enough worthless. At the last minute I decided I would go to the Post Office and enquire. When I was told its true worth I was dumbfounded. "Did you enjoy your holiday in Russia? Where did you go?" I came to my senses and explained to the cashier that I was exchanging the money for someone else. As I left the Post Office with £3000 weighing down my pockets I decided to celebrate. The first thing that I did was pay for another three weeks' stay in the hotel, and then I went to the pub and drank about four pints of Stella. I proceeded to the bookmakers, and after placing a few £50 bets on the horses and dogs I decided to have a go on the fixed odds betting terminals. In each bookmaker's there are four of these terminals, and each one is adapted to take £100 a spin, every twenty seconds. So, if you do your maths one could potentially lose £18,000 per hour but at that particular time I did not know any of this information. So as I took up my position and sat down in front of the terminal I began at first to only play £20 a spin on a game of roulette. Some spins I would win, but I lost far more. The adrenaline came and went; after each winning spin I was on a high, and it disappeared when I lost. I would then chase my losses to get my money back, and if I managed it I would convince myself that my luck was changing. And so in all circumstances I fed the money into the machine. I increased my stake to £100 a spin and within two hours I had lost over £1000. It must have caught the cashiers' attention because they kept looking knowingly at me. It wasn't until far later that I learnt of the cameras behind the monitors showing the staff how much the customer is betting.

After losing the £1000 I decided to get out of the shop and return to the pub. I drank pint after pint, and then I convinced myself that it I had only experienced a bad day at the bookmakers. That night I collapsed into bed exhausted from all off the day's activities. After having breakfast in the hotel I decided that I could easily regain the amount I'd lost the previous day, so I returned to the bookmakers. It was an almost exact repeat of the last visit. After spending three hours there I realised I'd gone through another £1000. These wretched machines were affecting my mood and at the same time were drawing me in like a bull to the matador's sword. I left the bookmakers dejected; how could I have squandered over £2000 in such a short period of time? How could I let a machine do this? This form of gambling was by far the most addictive form that I had ever come across, and the very next day I was back in the bookmakers convincing myself that my luck would change.

As I entered, the cashier immediately came across to me. "Would you like a free drink?" Obviously they had recognised that I was a keeper, and duly set about trying to make me feel as at home as possible. I took my seat once again. Surely this would be my day. I was not going to let a machine beat me. I left with £10 for a return ticket to Oxford.

When I left the bookmakers, tail between my legs, absolutely dejected I felt that I could not get much lower than this. How wrong I was. The very next day I was on the bus back to Oxford, and over the next five weeks I would wreak havoc on the colleges. My smash-and-grab approach was less successful than the first time, and what little I stole went straight into the machines. I was a man completely out of control, a rat trying to evade capture. It couldn't continue forever and sure enough the end was just around the corner. After around six weeks the inevitable happened.

It was on one of those trips back into Oxford that I found myself walking down a side road, when a car slowed down beside me. At first I thought this was strange, but when I looked into the car I recognised a C.I.D. officer who had arrested me once before. He recognised me immediately and as our eyes met he was out of the car and the chase was on. I was still confident I could escape but I was not as quick as I thought I was. I ran through an entrance to a shop and barged past everyone in my path. I noticed a staircase leading down so I grabbed hold of the banister and ran down. When I reached the bottom I frantically searched for an exit, but to no avail. As I looked around the C.I.D. officer was right behind me. He looked at me and said "Are you coming quietly?" and realising that the game was up I held out my two hands. Handcuffs on and rights read, then to the station. On the journey there the police officers seemed delighted that they had caught me, and even thanked me that they had lots of overtime to pay for their holidays from trying to capture me. At one point they said that at different times whilst I was on the run that they had C.I.D. officers sitting in college lodges monitoring cameras hoping that I would enter. The police always liked to get the last word in, but this did not occupy my thoughts, which were now on what story I could come up with that would get me out of all this. When we got to the police station we were greeted with a very cheerful atmosphere. It appeared word had got around that I had been caught, but I wasn't going to give them what they wanted straight away. The usual routine resumed; the police would ask a question and I would refuse to answer it.

The cell had no ventilation, and became extremely hot. But I would put the blanket over me and pretend that I was sleeping, showing the police that I didn't care. That was far from the truth; my mind was fixed on trying to remember all of my offences and come up with excuses and alibis. I was sure that the preparation would help me in court. An officer had warned me that the man in charge of my case was a Christian and would not give up. That meant nothing to me.

After being questioned for three days I went to the Magistrates' Court once again, and then the case was referred to the Crown Court. Throughout the following nine month process I was in remand at Bullingdon prison. Yo-yoing back and forth from prison to court can take its toll. I'd wake up at 6am, collect all my possessions, be taken to the prison reception to be stripped, searched and placed in a sweat box, then driven to court and wait in a cell for up to seven hours, then driven back to the prison, sometimes arriving as late as 8pm. And then going through the whole process again. All I wanted was to know the verdict so I could at least plan for the future.

I denied everything - even in crown court - but then the officer in charge of my case asked to see me in the court cells. I agreed, and he then presented to me the overwhelming evidence against me. I remember asking him "Officer, how can I help you?" With that offer the game was over. Over a period of around two weeks I informed the police about all of the offences that I could remember committing. In total I was charged with twelve burglaries and over 103 were taken in to consideration. The police seemed very pleased, and as far as I can remember the officer in charge of my case received a promotion.

I was informed before I had even been sentenced of what my prison term would be. I only met my barrister on the day of the sentencing; apparently he had been briefed beforehand by my lawyer. This was the way that things were done. He said very little, only asking for leniency considering that I had a severe gambling addiction and a two-year cocaine habit. I watched the Judge intently. He had his head down and it looked as though he was ignoring what my barrister was saying. And then he looked up and said that he had heard enough.

I was given a five year prison sentence. I was told that if I'd continued with my 'no comment' attitude I would have received seven to ten years. I was then taken down to the court cells and later that day I was transported to Bullingdon Prison to begin my sentence.

Back in Prison

So here I was once again. This sort of establishment was entirely familiar to me by now, and I knew I just had to get my head down and do my time. This started with a four hour wait in reception. When my name was finally called I was then told that I was to be escorted to a cell located on the A Wing. After a brief walk along the corridors of Bullingdon Prison I reached my cell. The prison officer unlocked the door, slammed it behind me and there I was once again, locked away from the outside world. As I was mulling over the length of my sentence and surveying my new home my eyes came to rest on a moving shape under the covers of one of the beds. He had been woken up by the slamming of the cell door and he was not happy. He informed me that this was his cell and that I was an unwelcome guest, and that I should get out. This was not an option; at least until the morning.

The man was sweating profusely, and although it was a hot day he clearly wasn't in a good way. Then I noticed he was shaking and I immediately thought to myself "Junkie." I knew that I had to act cautiously around someone who was almost definitely coming off heroin, so I got on with putting the sheets and blankets on the other bed. Then I put away what kit I had been given: a blue and white shirt, blue tee-shirt, jeans, pants, socks, towels and an information booklet. As I was doing this the guy looked up at me and asked "You got any tobacco?" I've never been a smoker so I just said that I couldn't help. At that moment he screamed and bent over, holding his stomach in obvious pain. "Are you ok mate?" I said.

"I ain't your mate. My name is Dan and I need my medicine."

Of course I knew that any heroin addict who was in prison would be prescribed a heroine substitute called methadone. This apparently helped those who were coming down from the drug, and it was obvious to me that Dan did indeed need his medicine. I also knew that he could shout and scream as much as he liked but he would not get anything until the dispensary was opened the next day. Another scream came from him and he began wriggling about, kicking his legs in the air and shouting. He didn't say another word to me but just stared straight at me all night. I resigned myself to staying awake; I did not want to turn my back on Dan for one second, and it was the most uncomfortable night I had ever encountered. Needless to say I didn't get a moment's sleep.

It was a relief when the cell door was unlocked at 7am, and after I had washed (using a bowl of water) I went to the wing office and spoke to the wing prison officer to tell him I wanted a cell change. I was fortunate; later on that day I got a move to another cell. The officers had obviously recognised that moving me in with a junkie was not beneficial for either of us. Under normal circumstances, when the prison was full (which it nearly always is,) it would never be possible to move. You'd just have to get on with it. As a result cellmates will fight each other and only then would the prison officers have to move someone to another cell for their own protection.

My new cellmate, John, was a lot more sociable. He was a little bit older than me. John was an old hand; he'd been through the system time and time again. It's sad but with the best intentions in the world, some people just keep coming back. More often than not their stories are tragic. John's story started in a broken home where his parents had been divorced. He was loathed by his step father, receiving no encouragement. His criminal record grew from stealing sweets from a shop, progressing right the way through to armed bank robbery, for which he was now serving a ten year sentence. He was a likeable character; he always seemed to be laughing, which was amazing considering the length of his sentence. To me it seemed unusual but the inmates who were serving the shorter sentences were often the ones who moaned. The ones who got the longer sentences just got on with it, and this was what John was doing. He was getting his head down and getting on with it, and I followed his example.

The first six weeks and the last six weeks in prison always seem to drag by. There are so many people in prison and so many going through the system that it takes about six weeks before you are given a job. In the meantime you are locked behind your cell door for around eighteen hours per day. Unlike my previous prison sentences there was a TV to ease the boredom there were now toilets in the cell, instead of plastic bottles.

I was given a job cleaning the wing, which was by now a good opportunity to get out of my cell so I accepted. I was told I would get £9 a week in wages which I could use on toiletries and the odd luxury such as sweets and fizzy drinks. After a while I enquired about education courses. I thought that if I could do something productive then I might be able to use it when I was released so I enrolled on

Numeracy and Literacy courses, but these enquiries actually led to an opportunity to work for St Giles Trust in the prison. This, in turn, opened another door so that I was able to work towards an NVQ 3 in Advice and Guidance. The role for St. Giles Trust involved having access to other wings in the prison. My job was to ascertain prisoners' needs and advocate for them. For example, someone might be on a short sentence, and being in prison means that they are unable to keep on top of rent payments. My job would be to try to get them some extra help so that they were less likely to feel as though they have to commit crime when got out. Under supervision I would advocate on their behalf to see what benefits would be available so that the rent was still being paid until they were released. At the time there was a scheme that enabled the benefits system to still pay the landlord even though someone was in prison for a maximum of twelve weeks, which really helped. This was just one example of what we did.

Obviously the role meant that a lot of trust was placed in us. While I was there, one man abused his position and was caught transferring drugs from one wing to another. He consequently lost his job and the privileges that had gone with it. The prison system is run by rewarding inmates for good behaviour. One of these rewards was having a job like the one I had, with considerable responsibility and far better pay than my cleaning position. I was even able to save a bit each week. Another reward was that I was eventually moved after six months from a double cell to a single cell, and for me this was the greatest prize. Although I had become friends with John he did have his moods from time to time (and he snored) and so I said my goodbyes to him. I later learnt that he'd been transferred to another prison anyway.

I found myself in the interesting position of being someone others could look to for help, and at the same time needing help myself. I had a prolific gambling addiction and as a consequence became a serial offender, and at no point (in any of my prison sentences) was I ever asked the question "Would you like help with your gambling addiction?" There was help offered to those who had alcohol or drug addictions, but not for those struggling with gambling. I found this astonishing. In fact, only since May 2015 has there been any type of help available but at the time of writing this is only in three prisons out of 150.

My responsibilities increased when I was given the opportunity to train to become a listener for the Samaritans. I was put on a rota with eleven other men and we were on call twenty four hours a day, seven days a week. We acted as a listening ear for those inmates who were not going to talk to the prison officers. It often meant I would be called out of my bed during the night to inmates' cells, or the hospital, or the block. Our role was to listen to fellow prisoners offloading their frustrations, from family matters to relationship problems, or just the frustration of being in prison. I just sat and listened; believe me when I say that there is an art to doing so. On many occasions I wanted to give advice but that was not my role so I used to give very brief replies. We did have meetings later on with the Samaritans at which we could offload our own problems, but no prison officers were present and the only time that they would be informed would be if there was a direct threat to someone's life.

After serving thirteen months in Bullingdon I was transferred to Springhill Open Prison where I was to serve the remaining seventeen months of my sentence. This prison was completely unlike the confined spaces and strict regime of Bullingdon. For starters it was open, with no walls so there was a freedom to walk around the grounds unescorted. This posed an unusual problem; it is easy to become convinced that it is possible to just walk out at any time, so it was an unfamiliar psychological challenge. When I arrived I was allocated a billet, sharing a room with another man. This time I was not locked in, but there were headcounts at various times during the day just to make sure that no one had walked straight out of the prison.

After about four weeks I was giving a cleaning job once again. For about six weeks I was tasked with cleaning the billet's shared bathroom and toilet facilities. The prison was set up with a reward system just like Bullingdon, and my goal was to be given a room of my own. After serving for about eight months I was informed that I was entitled to get a job outside the prison, and after all of the paperwork was done I was told given a job in Oxford working at Oxfam on the Cowley Road. I was dumbstruck - this was the very place that I had lived and the very place I had committed my crimes - but I had assumed that the prison knew what they were doing and I said nothing.

Twelve of us were taken from the prison in a white van, and at various points we were dropped off at our different places of work. So it was 9am and there I was, standing outside the shop in Oxford. I saw a man approach who introduced himself as the manager, and then I introduced myself as Ian from Springhill. We entered the shop and within two hours I was on the till taking cash and credit card payments. After just another hour the manager called me to his office and said that could I take the previous week's takings to the bank and so I found myself with £1300 in cash walking to the bank by myself less than two years after being sentenced in Oxford. It just seemed surreal, but I did the banking and then I returned to the shop. It was some weeks later when I was having my lunch on a bench on Magdalen Bridge that I noticed a man looking at me and I had uneasy feeling that he was in the police.

The next day as I was preparing to go back into Oxford I was pulled to one side by a prison officer and told that I would not be returning to Oxfam. My uneasy feeling on the bridge was accurate; a prison officer confirmed that the police officer had suggested that under the circumstances it would be inappropriate for me to return to the scene of my crimes. About a week later I was back in the van, this time headed for the Age Concern shop in Aylesbury. This job was totally different. I was in the basement of the shop sorting and steam-ironing all of the clothes that had been donated by the public. I had an hour-long break for lunch, during which I used to wander around Friars Square Shopping Centre, often just sitting on a bench watching the world go by. After another six months had passed I was nearing the point of release and more opportunities came my way. I was now entitled to home leave but unfortunately for me I had no home to go to so I had to stay on site. It was hard watching others go home. These people were also lucky enough to be permitted to bring in a car, so they could travel easily between home and prison.

I was now a week away from being released. I was informed that accommodation had been found for me in Aylesbury. This town was to become my new home. As part of my release plan I was to be on license for thirty months, and to start with I was to report to a probation officer three times per week as a classified Prolific and Priority Offender.

Then it was time. I reported to the reception area and I was given a bus ticket, £50 and a set of documents to give to my probation officer. And that was it. I walked down the hill by the prison and I caught the bus to Aylesbury. I was now going to a town in which I knew no one and I found myself alone once more. My only guaranteed company were the probation officer and my allocated police officer. Despite all of these concerns I soon settled into my new town. Over time the probation officer visits became less frequent. It appeared that the experience of the last two and a half years – the conditions, the dangers and the unending boredom – had done little to override my instinct to gamble, and before long I was itching to get back to the betting shops.

Before this could really take hold again, though, I was taken extremely ill.

Hospital

One night not long after leaving prison, I was lying on my bed and I started to shake uncontrollably. As I came round I stood up and looked down at the sheets, which were soaked with sweat. I felt sick and couldn't stop trembling. At first I assumed it was flu, and decided that the best thing to do would be to try to sleep it off.

The next morning I had a visit from one of the housing workers, who just took one look at me and said "I'm getting an ambulance." There was no hesitation. Her face told me instantly that I was in a serious state. At first the paramedics were reluctant to take me in case I infected the ward, as symptoms included diarrhoea and vomiting. However by then I was experiencing tremendous pain in my right leg and that was the point at which they decided I needed emergency treatment. I was taken to Stoke Mandeville Hospital and as I arrived the symptoms began to become more severe. I was escorted into the waiting room, and began shaking so much as they wheeled me through the hospital. Doctors suddenly seemed to be appearing from all directions, and one of them asked me whether I'd taken on drugs or alcohol, and whether I'd eaten anything in the last 24 hours. I hadn't.

When another doctor noticed black spots on my hands I was rushed to an isolation ward. I was given a cocktail of drugs and began slipping in and out of consciousness. A drip was placed in my arm and the nurses were coming in and out of my room like bees collecting pollen on a hot summer's day. I then became uncomfortably hot. I felt the sweat pouring off me and the bed sheets were soaking wet within minutes of being changed. The pain in my leg was becoming unbearable. My lowest point came during the night when I needed to go to the toilet. I dragged myself off of the bed and was making my way across the room, but I didn't make it. I found myself lying in the middle of the bathroom on the floor surrounded by my own waste. I was so close to tears at that point, but I found the courage to pull the emergency cord and within seconds the nurse arrived. Imagine the scene as the nurse entered the toilet. But to her absolute credit she looked at me and said "Let's get you washed up and back in to bed."

Later on I found that I had lost the feeling in my right leg. It was frightening because however much my brain told my leg to move, my leg ignored it. The doctors didn't seem concerned though; they just told me to raise my leg. Obviously this was impossible as it was completely unresponsive and kept flopping back down. It was on one of these occasions that I heard a doctor say that I might have suffered a stroke. After conducting further tests they decided to transfer me to another hospital in High Wycombe. They thought that I had had a stroke and that it was affecting my heart, so more tests were carried out. As all of this was happening I was drifting in and out of consciousness.

I was now surrounded by other people who seemed to have heart defects of one kind or another. The constant bleeping of the heart monitors will stay for me forever. While I was lying on my bed one day the curtains around me were closed by a nurse, but I could just see through the gap between them, and people were gathering around the bed opposite mine. The curtain was opened again around an hour later, and I noticed that the bed was now empty. Within the next hour another person was in the same bed as the person who had died. It made me realise how fragile life is, and how many people are put through this system every day.

The results from all of the tests that I had undergone came back, and I was told by a consultant that I had the symptoms of Infective Endocarditis (IE) caused by Staphylococcus. The symptoms of acute IE usually begin suddenly with high fever (102°–104°F), fast heart rate, fatigue, and rapid, intensive valve disease. I was then also told that I had blood poisoning. I remembered getting a new tattoo six weeks earlier, and assumed that was where I had picked it up. Before I could get my thoughts straight I was whisked off to a third hospital: Hammersmith, where I was to have open-heart surgery in the morning. I was informed that they were going to fit a St. Jude mechanical heart valve in to the aortic valve to allow the blood to flow freely around the heart. They did not want a blood clot. That could have been instantly fatal. I was told I would be undergoing heart surgery in the morning, and that I could not eat or drink anything. A nurse came around and shaved my chest. Every hour or so new faces would appear around my bed all asking the same question: "Can we look at your hands?" The junior doctors had obviously got word that I had black spots on my hands, which apparently is very rare and usually only seen in textbooks. I was obviously becoming something of a celebrity to the young doctors. After they had left I lay on my bed taking in my surroundings and watching all kinds of visitors coming and going, delivering fruit and flowers to their loved ones. I had no visitors, and at that point I felt lonely. I didn't usually show any kind of emotion, but this day was an exception. The intense lights of the ward were hurting my eyes and I was starting to feel very irritable, constantly tossing from side to side with the sweat pouring. The nurse noticed again and came across to administer me some more drugs, and I quickly drifted off into an uncomfortable night's sleep.

I awoke to the sounds of activity all around me; the nurses were waking patients up and a lady brought breakfast. The murmurings of people waking up were echoing throughout the ward - a cough here and a sneeze there – ushering in a new day. Today was the day of my operation. A nurse approached my bed and gave me a hospital gown to put on and before I knew it I was on my way.

On the way to the preparation room before surgery I thought to myself "I am a piece of meat. If I die, I die."

A team of three performed the operation. They all seemed very well drilled, like a clockwork machine, and despite the few attempts needed to get the anaesthetic into me, the whole thing appeared effortless. For some reason I was determined that the anaesthetic wouldn't beat me; I didn't want to be overcome by anything. But one of the doctors instructed me to count backwards from ten. I reached seven and was out for the count.

I remember feeling extreme discomfort as I came round. My neck had been pulled right back into an unnatural angle, but as I tried to move I heard a nurse whisper in my ear to be still. That egged me on, and I tried even harder, but my body just wasn't doing as it was told. A few minutes later I felt a tube being pulled out of my mouth, and with a cough I was put into a sitting position on the bed and told to relax. In that state of groggy anaesthesia I had no choice.

After a week or so I was transferred to the main ward. As is typical after open heart surgery, my appetite didn't return for about four days. The nurses gave me some really good advice about heart disease, and made me feel secure. They helped me not to worry about the stitches coming out – a thought which was proving difficult to shift. It was hard for the first few weeks; my body had taken a hammering and it took time to recover from any activity. Just going to have a shower was a mission in itself. I would shuffle towards the room at such a snail's pace an onlooker would have thought I was a hundred years old, and when I finally made it I struggled to lift my good leg into the shower, but the reward justified the effort. I had been longing for a hot shower, and as I soaked in the spray of the water I felt clean once again. The long journey back to bed took at least as long, and I invariably collapsed, exhausted.

In the bed next to mine was a man called Raj. After talking to him for a while I learnt that he was 53 and that he had previously been in hospital for a heart operation but now there were complications. He informed me after one particular conversation that he had been a champion 100m runner for India. This man showed me such kindness because he had noticed that I did not receive any visitors, and he would often get his family to bring me in pieces of fruit. This was a fantastic break from hospital food, especially as his family would then come and sit around me and talk during visiting hours. Raj was moved to another ward some days later and I did not see him again, but I will always remember him.

My rehabilitation seemed to be going slow, but I was getting stronger week by week. I remember on one occasion being taken by one of the nurses for a walk up some stairs, and as I got half way up the nurse stopped and said "Do you hear that? It sounds like a watch or a clock." And indeed I could hear it, but we were both mystified as to where the noise was coming from. Then it dawned on me that the ticking sound was coming from my own chest. How extraordinary! It was the mechanical device that they had inserted into the aortic valve. I now could hear my own heart. We both burst out laughing.

Then after about four weeks of intensive antibiotics I started to get the feeling back in my right leg. Soon after that I was able to walk again – slowly at first – but my spirits took off. The drugs were still affecting me though; within ten minutes of them being injected into my blood stream I felt as though I was on a boat in the middle of the sea in choppy waters. This made me want to be sick. The doctors had decided that it would be best to inject the antibiotics straight into my blood stream, and as a consequence I had a small insertion made into the side of my chest into which they placed a tube. I was awake when this procedure took place and I was astonished as I looked at the tube itself. It was as long as my arm, but within minutes it was painlessly inserted. Once the tube was in place there was no need for any new needles.

One morning as I looked across the ward I noticed a man being put into a bed. It looked like he was being escorted by prison officers, and as he lay down his hand and foot were handcuffed to the bed. As I shuffled across the ward to introduce myself I was intercepted by the prison officer and told not to talk to the man. I felt sorry for him, although I did not know what offence or offences he had committed. I am not sure of what other option there was for the authorities, but I couldn't help thinking he should be treated with some level of dignity. I was reminded of my recent past and ongoing contact with the probation officer. Apparently they had visited me with a police officer from time to time but I have no recollection of any visits, such was the state that I was in.

It was a few days after the operation that one of the nurses told me to lift up my gown. "That's odd..." I thought. He instructed me to take a deep breath, at which point I really began to wonder what was about to occur. Then he reached down and pulled out the catheter which I hadn't even known was in. They must have inserted it before I went in for the operation, without me knowing about it. Anyway, I saw its removal as a sign that I must have been getting better.

***

I only went to church because I couldn't stand listening to the heart monitors any longer. The constant beep... beep... beep was enough to drive even the most steady of souls to madness, and it drove mine downstairs to the chapel. As I entered the chapel a woman greeted me. She looked like a vicar, and with a cheerful disposition and a huge smile she welcomed me into the chapel. Then a man approached and introduced himself as the vicar's husband. He also had a manner which made me feel most welcome. Then in came an old lady, being pushed in her wheelchair by a nurse. That was everyone! The congregation that morning was a small one but that didn't distract from the atmosphere. I recognised that this place, and those in it, had been filled with peace. The chapel itself was unassuming; a small room with about 30 chairs positioned in a half moon surrounded a rostrum where the vicar stood. She conducted a short service, and as she was speaking I noticed a ray of sunshine shimmer across the room. To me that felt significant.

After the service the vicar came across again and thanked me for my "wonderful singing." I was flabbergasted as I am pretty sure my singing resembles the sound of a fog horn emanating through the mist on a cold dark night, but I took the compliment. She then said lots of people will have enjoyed it. I did a quick calculation and unless my sums were wrong there were only five of us in total. "Lots of people?" I thought. It turns out I had been on hospital radio.

Then the woman did something that would change the course of my life: she placed a wooden cross into my hand.

Journey to Faith

I returned to life in the outside world, renting a small room in a shared house. I was still weak but each day I was getting a little stronger. At first the very idea of walking just a short distance to go to the corner shop was too much. It would take me an hour and a half; I would have to stop every ten minutes or so to could catch my breath and take a rest. On a normal day the same journey would have taken me just fifteen minutes. But with each trip to the shops I became stronger, and over time I began to feel fitter. As I started to walk further I became able to attend the probation office, and to take the occasional trip into Aylesbury, and more importantly I was getting fresh air instead of sitting in my room.

After a short time I received some good news: I had been granted a council flat. A body of evidence from my probation officer, the police, and my doctor hastened the whole process, and I was sent straight to the top of the waiting list. I was extremely grateful and excited; at last I would have a place of my own that I could call home. I viewed the ground floor flat which was only a stone's throw away from where I was already living and I immediately accepted the flat. I moved in within six weeks. I managed to acquire furniture from various charitable organisations, and one of the probation officers accompanied me around some shops to help. The probation office even contributed some of the money I needed for some of the furnishings.

It can be quiet lonely living a flat, and I had been warned not to return to Oxford by the police, so although I had a good home I had no real friends. I felt isolated, and sometimes angry with whole situation. Every two weeks I would have to claim Jobseeker's Allowance at the Job Centre, and in order to receive my money I would have to show evidence that I had applied for jobs. I was excited at the prospect of finding work - after all I felt as though I had changed and I had a collection of qualifications from prison that would surely help me in the whole job seeking process. How wrong I was. Not a single employer responded to any letter or email that I sent in over two years. I became despondent, but rather than give up I decided to go on a computer course. This took me over a year to complete and at the end I received a certificate declaring that I was now 'computer literate' by European standards. This achievement helped me to keep my chin up.

It was when I was feeling low that an idea returned to my head: gambling. I'd almost forgotten about it until that point, and I had been looking forward to a clean start. But here I was again, often left with no money (and therefore no food.) It was my probation officer who told me that the Vineyard Church provides food parcels, and because I was in need I went along. This became a weekly occurrence: I would gamble away all of my Jobseeker's Allowance, and it was just as well that I was unable to get my housing benefit money or I would have gambled that away too. It was on a trip to get a food parcel that a man approached, and immediately befriended me. He introduced himself as Mark, the assistant pastor at Aylesbury Vineyard Church. He asked if he could talk to me, and just sat back as I unleashed all of my frustration at him. He listened to my tales of woe, and after I had finished I slumped into the armchair. I was used to being asked probing questions by authorities trying to trip me up, but Mark behaved differently. He listened to me without interrupting or criticizing, and when I had eventually finished he started to talk. He talked about how I was looking for fulfilment in all the wrong places, and that I needed Jesus. This made (a little) sense to me, so before I left he gave me a little booklet called 'Why Jesus?' and another called "What's the point." As I left the vineyard that day I felt a little lighter on my feet as if a weight had been lifted.

It was a few days later that I sat back in my flat and I began to read through the booklets, and it was on one particular page that I became stuck and that was the believer's prayer. What this was offering was extraordinary: it was saying that Jesus came for our sins and he took the sins of the world on him. He died and he rose on the third day and the shedding of his blood reconciled us back with God, and that you and I will be forgiven and we can have eternal life if we truly accept him as our saviour. This image of a God who suffers with people struck me, and I wanted to know more.

In the weeks that followed I returned to the vineyard and had many more conversations with Mark: about life, Christianity and Jesus. I had even been given a role in the church, delivering furniture to people around the town from what they called 'The Storehouse', and I spent most of my time meeting new people and talking to them. It was fantastic. I even started to go to church on a Sunday, which was a completely new experience.

The first time, I stood at the back of the school assembly hall and simply observed what was going on. My initially thoughts were that this was some kind of cult. There was a woman dancing with a scarf twirling around her and people were singing with their hands above their heads. This seemed like crazy behaviour to me, and at that time I certainly could not understand it. But I was intrigued and curious. I then started to read more from the booklets, but also from a Bible I had been given. I began a conversation with God in the privacy of my own flat, but at this early stage I didn't want to pray publically. Then I started to wrestle with God: I would say "Ok, I will give you 60% of my life as long as I can keep 40%." I felt an inaudible voice inside me say quiet clearly: "It's all or nothing." I didn't exactly know what 40% of my life would have included, but I knew there were certain things I wanted to keep for myself.

I also began doing odd jobs helping out here and there at the Vineyard, and I did consider a few people my friends. But still at the back of my mind I knew there was something missing. It was around this time that I joined the Healing on the Streets ministry team. This was a team whose aim was to demonstrate Jesus' love in a non-confrontational way. I saw people give to utter strangers, whether they were homeless, hungry, isolated or lonely. I was beginning to see that this Jesus was real, and the evidence had been staring me straight in the face all of the time. The light switch had been turned on and I had got it at last: Jesus is real and alive and working in those who believe in him and his arms are open to everyone. We prayed for people, and saw people healed. Often those people had the same basic need as I did – to know Jesus and devote their lives to him. Seeing this was the final straw.

On 31st March 2010 I got on my knees and gave the remaining 40% of my life to Jesus. As I looked at the clock at the side of my bed it was 8:45pm. I then closed my eyes and opened them again, and it was 6.30am. I don't know where those hours went, but I am drawn to the idea that I was resting in the arms of God.

"Anyone who believes in Christ is a new creation, the old has gone and the new has come."

When I woke up I was so excited that I needed to tell as many people as I could about Jesus. I remember walking down the road but feeling like I was walking on water. And the hedges had a smell to them I had never smelt before. The whole world had taken on a new lease of life. I burst through the Vineyard doors and announced the news to everyone. This happened on Good Friday.

In the months that followed I continued to volunteer at The Vineyard. I began to pray for people and I immersed myself in the Bible. I wanted to know everything required in order to tell people about Jesus; I just couldn't stop myself! From strangers in the park to train ticket inspectors, I had to tell everyone. I had a spring in my step and a hope and a future.

On the 30th May that year I was baptised in a school swimming pool. The night before I just could not sleep. I knew that that morning there would be four of us who would give our testimony and then would be baptised and a bring-and-share meal would be had by all. I began worrying about what I would say in front of the church. Would I get all muddled up and start to stutter and make a real fool of myself? I then decided to write everything down on a piece of paper – my background and how I had come to this decision. I took a couple of hours but afterwards I was prepared as I could be.

The school hall was packed. It looked to me as though the whole town had come out, which only added to my anxiety. Then Mark got up and preached about baptism. The time seemed to fly by and suddenly I was up. All four of us were called to the front and one by one we gave our testimonies. When my name was called I stepped forward and I need not have worried; the words just seemed to flow. I did not once have to refer to any of the notes that I had written down. Then we all went into to the swimming pool, and were asked questions that would confirm that we accepted Jesus into our lives. I said "Yes!" I remember being tipped backwards and totally submerged in the water. I felt a real sense of peace, and as I was brought back to the surface the feeling was that of being totally clean. After we had all been baptised the congregation got changed and went swimming before eating lunch together. The day was one that I will never forget. I sent a card to my probation officer and the police also telling them of my new found faith. I never received a reply.

Most people that I came into contact with accepted that I had now become a Christian, but some were more sceptical, just waiting for me to fall or make a mistake so they could say "Told you so." There's a saying that a leopard never changes his spots. The only way of proving I had changed was to act like it. I could talk all I wanted, but I needed to make sure that over the coming years I was walking the walk. In the months that followed I continued to volunteer at the vineyard and something amazing happened there. I received prayer for my gambling, and I experienced a dark cloud-like a mist leave my body and move along the wall and out of the building. I told Mark and Dave, another friend from church, what I saw and they prayed for me more, and for the next eighteen months I was able to stop gambling completely.

In the August of 2010 I went to a Christian festival called New Wine, which is held for a fortnight at the Royal Bath and West Showground in Somerset. I was attending one of the talks in the main venue, and it was during the worship before the talk that I looked around me and I could see grown men weeping and some women crying out and shaking. A single thought crossed my mind: "I am a man and I don't cry." And with that the inaudible voice said "That's interesting to know." Before I could have time to process the thought I began to weep uncontrollably. It was if all my past hurts were being emptied out. After I had gained some control of myself I sat down feeling slightly tired but also, curiously enough, at peace. To be honest I don't remember much about the speaker or even what he was saying, but what I certainly remember is what happened next. At the end of the talk we were all asked whether we would like to go up to the front for prayer. I decided I would. While someone was praying for me I felt what I firmly believe to be the presence of the Holy Spirit. I immediately fell backwards and someone caught me. I felt a warm sensation moving throughout my body and I began to shake and cry, and feel joy and peace. It was incredible. There were now several people around me praying, and they were putting oil on my forehead and legs. I had never experienced anything like this before but I had a sense that it was okay. I must have been on that floor for at least thirty minutes. At one point I opened my eyes to see Mark there with what looked like a beaker of water. This reassured me that what I was experiencing was safe and that I need not be afraid. Of course, Mark was not there at all. Then I heard a voice say "We'd better get him off the floor as the next speaker is arriving soon." With that I was lifted to my feet and given a free coffee coupon. I didn't need a bonus after that experience, but a coffee certainly didn't go amiss.

I felt a real sense of love and peace at New Wine. I was sitting in the market place drinking that complementary cup of coffee when I noticed a disabled child being pushed by a woman. At that point I felt a strong impulse telling me to go over and pray for the child – not for anything specific. I resisted and said to myself that it would not be right for a man to approach a woman and a child. However the desire to pray for this child persisted.

I should not have worried; another opportunity was given to me. I was this time walking in the alley behind the market place and as I looked up I saw the same woman and child. Immediately the Holy Spirit prompted me to pray for the child. I walked past the woman, and started coming up with all types of excuses not to pray for the child. Then I did a U-turn. At precisely the same moment the woman also turned around, and, still resistant, I passed her again. I walked to the end of the alley and turned around, and the same thing happened again. I then decided that I needed one more sign, so I told God that I would pray for the child if a man walked past wearing a red t-shirt. He did, and still I was still not satisfied. I asked once more that I would turn around again and for a man to be in a red t-shirt, and as I did a man entered the alley. It seemed as though no one else was around him, and he was wearing a completely red t-shirt. Of course, whether that was God or chance it was just the prompt I need.

As I approached them my mouth felt dry, and everything seemed to be in slow motion. As calmly as I could, I asked whether I could pray for the child, and to my astonishment the woman said yes. I knelt so that I was on eye-level as the child, and as I looked into her eyes they were the most beautiful eyes that I had ever looked at. I prayed that she would be free from the contraption that supported her, and that she would be able to run around with boys and girls of her own age. I prayed all of this in Jesus' name, and with that the girl went whizzing down the alley in her contraption. Then the woman said to me that her girl was extremely unsettled that morning, as if she was waiting for something. After I returned to my tent I relayed the story to some of the group and later on to some people at Aylesbury Vineyard.

As I lay on my bed that night I felt the Holy Spirit guide me through everything that had happened and I went to sleep happy in the knowledge that I had stepped out in faith and done the right thing.

Servanthood

Early in my new life I learnt that to serve others is an essential part of Christian activity. Jesus said "Love the Lord your God with all your heart, mind, body and strength" and "Love your neighbour as you would love yourself." Those instructions were instrumental to my growing understanding. I had only ever taken from society, and now it was time to start giving.

I began to volunteer for the church working on the van delivering furniture to those families in need. This enabled me to reach out and serve the local community. On Tuesday and Thursday mornings The Vineyard would open to the general public and those who are in need could come along and choose furniture, clothes and food items from the Storehouse. Once they had chosen what they wanted, they were put on a waiting list. After about a two week wait we would go to their homes and deliver what they had asked for. This was a good opportunity to show real love in a practical way, and it was also a chance to engage with new people from different backgrounds and cultures. While The Vineyard is extremely good at reaching out to the local community, they never force religion on anyone. Prayer is offered when people first come to the Storehouse, and if someone accepts that offer that's great, but if not then their preference is respected. It's about loving people regardless of circumstance or situation. After being isolated and lonely on many different occasions I felt like I really understood the importance of human contact, so I fell naturally into the role and loved it.

As I spent longer working for The Vineyard, they began to trust me with different roles; often roles which needed a lot of empathy and wisdom. I had direct contact with people in need, from drug users to homeless people, and I was able to use my own past experiences to help whoever was in front of me. Not long after my arrival we were informed that we could be moving to a bigger building with much more space for the Storehouse, and that the church would no longer need to use the school assembly hall on Sundays. This was exciting news.

Around this time I met a woman and we started a relationship. She just happened to be a nurse who worked at the surgery where I had my blood taken each week. I entered the relationship purely following my own emotions, without really considering how compatible we were. My heart overruled my mind. She had her own house in a different town and I would often spend weekends rambling through the countryside with her and her dog. She also started to attend The Vineyard and everyone knew us. She followed a similar path to my own, in that she decided to follow Jesus and become baptised. As the relationship developed over the coming months we grew ever closer to one another, which resulted in me given up my flat and possessions and moving in with her. When Mark found out he was mortified, and asked "What are you doing moving in with your sister?" I did not completely understand this comment but over the coming months I would.

The church relocation took around three months to complete. When I visited the new premises the first thing that struck me was that it was huge. The previous tenants had been a local college training organisation, and as I was shown around the enormity of the task ahead hit me. This would need a lot of people doing a lot of work, but I was up for it, and the enthusiasm showed by so many people was an inspiration to see. At the helm of this project were Mick and Lynn: the senior pastors, and Mark and Viv: the assistant pastors. We were able to save a lot of money by pooling our skills, like Mark's previous life as a building surveyor for the council and Mick's former job as a plumber. It was an ideal collection of people for that job.

As soon as the keys were handed over the work began. I found myself there nearly every day doing numerous tasks that needed to be done. These ranged from gathering all the six foot tall grass that had been cut down at the front of the building, copious weeding (which took an age,) digging holes in the concrete, laying carpets down in the what would be the pastors' offices, sweeping the floor in the main auditorium, painting the walls, and that was just the start. This time spent at the building not only was good for my self-esteem but I was also finally doing something that I truly believed in (and, of course, there were plenty of sandwiches and cakes to hold my attention.) A swarm of people helped to get the building ready, and some months later we were able to have the first service: a brilliant and well attended day. It was incredible to see so many people gathered together to celebrate God's provision and love.

I witnessed first-hand the love and compassion shown to everyone and anyone; in the pouring rain and in the sunshine men and women were giving up their time to selflessly reach out to those who were in need of help. The church then prayed that I would get a full time paid job, which I did, and at the time of writing I am still there.

Not long after the move my relationship was thrown into jeopardy. Within months of moving into a new area the thoughts of gambling came flooding back. The temptation became too much, and so after eighteen gambling-free months I gave in. Like most gamblers I kept it a secret, and hid away my habit. Often I couldn't wait until the church service was over just so that I could get back to the bookmakers. I was only gambling a few pounds at a time to start with, but this rapidly got out of hand. I applied for a £4000 loan online and it was accepted. At the same time as the gambling was taking hold I proposed to my partner and got engaged, with the wedding planned for the February of 2012. I continued to gamble, often making excuses to my work that I was sick and getting on a bus to a nearby town. I was back on the fixed odds betting terminals and the money ran out within two months. My mind was yet again thrown into turmoil: what was I doing? How could I pay for this? I applied for yet another loan - this time £3700 - and again it was accepted. All the time I was telling myself I could get out of trouble and win back what I had lost, but within a month I had lost all of the money again. I then maxed out two credit cards with a combined limit of £2500, leaving me with a debt of £10,200. I was refused further loans, and it was at that point that I realised how far I had fallen. I felt ashamed and stupid. I eventually told my fiancée. As a result the relationship broke down, and I had to leave.

***

I had a dream in which I found myself high up in what looked like a cell, and as I looked down from my vantage point I saw an angel sitting on a cold stone, sobbing. It had a chain attached to it. I could not see the angel's face, which was covered by a wing. As I looked up I saw bars across the top of the cell wall and through the bars it was dark with flickering stars. My own breath was visible, such was the cold. Then the dream ended. I found the following passage in the bible some months later and I immediately recalled the dream:

"Though you already know this, I want to remind you that the Lord delivered his people out of Egypt, but later destroyed those who did not believe. And the angels who did not keep their positions of authority but abandoned their own home - these he has kept in darkness, bound with everlasting chains for judgement on the great day."

One morning I woke up and I could smell sick on my bed sheets, but I had not been sick. Another passage immediately came to my mind.

"Of them the proverbs are true: "A dog returns to its vomit," and, "A sow that is washed returns to her wallowing in the mud."

This was certainly the case for me at that precise moment in time. I had returned to my old lifestyle and I believe that I was being shown the error of my ways. I asked myself the question "Why did I do what I did even after I gave my life to Jesus?" Again I found an answer in scripture:

"Be alert and of sober mind. Your enemy the devil prowls around like a roaring lion looking for someone to devour."

I came to the conclusion that the rekindling of my addiction had been the result of this kind of attack. I was vulnerable at that time, what with my recent move. Nobody would know if I nipped into the bookmakers, so I did it. I believe the devil had a hand in this. I was being tempted, and unfortunately for me I took the bait. After that I was taunted by the illusion that now I was in debt the only solution was to try and gamble my way out of it.

Thankfully I had the support of my friends at The Vineyard, who reminded me that there is no condemnation for God's children. They brought back to me the realisation that Jesus' death and resurrection makes him victorious over all evil.

I left my ex-fiancées home a broken man. So much was lost that I felt as though I had gone twelve rounds with the heavyweight champion of the world and then been challenged to step back into the ring. I was confused and exhausted, and suicidal thoughts began to worm their way into my mind.

Jesus had not given up, though. Unknown to me a Christian couple had approached Mark two weeks earlier and asked him what they could do for Ian?

I simultaneously rang Mark and came clean about everything. He was clear that he thought I had messed up, but I didn't feel at all judged. Then he said that a Christian family who just happen to live in the same town had offered to help me. After a quick phone call he told me that they had offered me a room in their house to stay for a while, and so that same day I collected all of my belongings and moved in with my new-found family. The stay was initially for a month, but over the coming years I was to learn such a lot. God had not abandoned me, despite my recent diversion. It was a slow road to recovery, but I was determined that this new chance would not be missed.

Back on Track

I was a broken man. Never had I felt this hopeless. I seemed always on the brink of tears and the slightest thoughts about my descent back into gambling sparked ever deeper depression. I was tempted to slip back into my life of crime, and sometimes the thought of ending my life crossed my mind. Yet during this dark time I felt a closeness to God that I had somehow ignored before. I was reading my Bible, I was praying and I certainly could feel the presence of God. I knew that without the strength God was giving me I would not have been able to carry on. This was a wakeup call; there were lessons to be learnt, and I had to get my life back on track immediately.

From the first day that I set my alarm for 5am, I had a routine and I was determined to stick to it. I would get up, get dressed, pray and have breakfast. I'd leave the house at 6am and walk the fifteen minutes to work, which started at 6.30am. My job was to work on different types of machines in a furniture factory. The machines themselves did all kinds of things, from boring holes to edging and cutting into sides of wardrobes, bedside cabinets and various other furniture that was destined for universities, military establishments, Butlins and other establishments across the country.

My job was extremely tedious and repetitive. The view that I had from my machine was of white-washed breeze blocks. That was all I saw all day, except during a ten minute tea break in the morning, a half an hour break for lunch and another ten minute break at 5.20. On most days I worked until 8.30pm, and I also worked most Saturdays.

By the time I got home I just went to my room and collapsed into bed. That was my routine for months on end.

For the first three months my mind was in turmoil, but I still went to church. Over that period three different people came up to me and on different occasions told me to "Be courageous." At that time I did not really know what they meant but I always acknowledged and thanked the person for telling me this, and after the second person said the same thing I was intrigued. And when a third repeated the advice I was flabbergasted. I couldn't stop thinking about the words.

It was also around this time that I had a heart-to-heart talk with Phil – my new host - and I was amazed at how wise and gentle and loving this man was. When he wanted to talk to me he would say "Ian, how are things with you, life and the universe." At those words I knew a proper talk was imminent. On this occasion we sat down and talked about setting up something called an accountability partner. He explained that it was important for me to have someone who I could talk to about anything, and this made real sense to me because it would enable me to get off my chest my concerns. So Phil agreed to be my accountability partner.

I was also to speak the truth at all times. After all, Jesus said that the truth sets us free. I agreed with Phil that I would speak the truth at all times, and that I would do so from that point on. Remember, to a gambler like me, dishonestly had become second nature, so speaking out this declaration was pivotal in freeing me from lying. This was a big step forward.

The next stage of being accountable was to relinquish all of my finances to Phil. This included credit cards, debit cards, cheque books, everything. He would hold onto these until such a time that I had proven that I could manage my own finances. This was agreed. We also looked at my bank statement online and printed off six months of my transactions, and it certainly was not good reading. I know this sounds crazy but I was surprised even though I knew the huge amount of debt that I was in. To see it on a statement was shocking.

In order to become a good steward of my finances I have needed discipline. I am now in control of my spending, but I need safeguards in place. The Bible calls this 'self-discipline.' The safeguards include the agreement that I won't buy any kind of raffle or lottery ticket or enter competitions with prizes, using the menu on the TV so I don't see horse racing while channel-hopping, and avoiding national newspapers which advertise sports gambling. Finally, and most importantly of all, I thank God every time I pass a bookmaker's, for taking gambling away from me.

It was around three months later that Phil said to me "Ian, there's a conference at St Pauls in Hammersmith run by New Wine and Christian Vision for Men called 'Courageous.' Would you like to go?" Immediately those words 'be courageous' came to me: the words that had been given to me over three different times. I immediately replied "Yes!"

I remember staring at the stained glass windows, radiant in the sunlight which flickered through the tinted panes. As I stood next to Phil, around ten men began to beat on the drums, which was strangely uplifting. And then everyone stood up and began singing one of the songs that was on a sheet we had be given. The hairs on the back of my head stood on end. After we had finished singing a representative of New Wine took to the stage to talk. After he had finished he invited us to the front of the church. Then he asked us to turn to someone nearby and introduce ourselves and pray for each other. So that was exactly what I did: I introduced myself to the man next to me, and then I asked him what was on his heart and what would he like prayer for. He said that he felt compelled to help those who were abused and traded by Human Traffickers and I prayed into this area for him.

He then started to pray for me and I felt the Holy Spirit speak to me powerfully. The conviction was this: I had to help gambling addicts. I had to find a way of playing my part in freeing people from the grip of gambling. I was bemused. Gambling had destroyed my life, so who was I to talk? How could I possibly make a difference? All of this was swimming around in my mind, but when I relayed what had happened to Phil I am sure that he could see that there was a real change in me.

I sat down for the afternoon session and a man called Carl Beech, President of Christian Vision for Men took to the stage. He was talking about a section in scripture about a king and a knife. The king's name was Gilead but apart from that I remember very little. My mind was elsewhere. It was some years later that I met Carl and had lunch and discussed gambling with him.

On the journey home I felt rejuvenated; now I had a purpose and a goal. I began talking to Phil about everything that had happened. I mumbled on about how we could bring an end to online gambling, as I was sure that a lot of people were suffering because of the impact that it was having. But next to me was the voice of reason: Phil is an internet security expert, so he knew that to stop online gambling was a virtual impossibility. That reality check did not dampen my enthusiasm.

When we returned home my mind was working overtime. Over the next week I kept wondering where to start with my new-found purpose. Then one afternoon I got down on my knees and I began praying, and while I was praying I had a vision. In front of me I saw a betting office, and it was as though I was viewing the scene from the front door. Along the left-hand side of the wall were four fixed odds betting terminals, and on each screen there was a golden key. I then saw Jesus. I did not see his face but I somehow knew it was him. Next to him were four teenagers and standing behind the counter was a woman. It looked as though the teenagers were being asked to leave. Then I heard a voice say "Stay within the law," and the vision ended.

I immediately began work finding out as much about the gambling industry as possible, and over the following months I trawled the internet. Some useful information quickly emerged. Firstly, the bookmakers were only allowed four fixed odds betting terminals in each shop. I personally knew the amounts of money that these machines could take: £100 every twenty seconds, which is up to £18,000 per hour. An individual's life can be ruined in one hour by one of their machines, as well as the lives of their family. I had experienced those consequences, but never appreciated the speed at which it could happen. I later read that the media had dubbed these machines 'the crack cocaine of gambling' and I learnt through intensive research that the bookmakers target poorer areas of the country to take advantage of gambling's addictive properties. A charity that highlighted this was immediately closed down and their funding was withdrawn. The bookmakers play a very clever game. Because they are only allowed four machines in each shop they open more shops, hence more unrest in communities as gamblers often lose their temper in fits of rage after losing money on the machines.

I later met Matt Zarb-Cousins from fairergambling, who wrote a piece for The Guardian about fixed odds betting terminals. They advocate a reduction from £100 a spin to £2 a spin. Even though there is a lot of support for this from councils in England and Wales, the government have only reduced the amount to £50 a spin. This is still far too high and so the campaign continues.

I also found out that two main companies supplied these terminals throughout the country to the bookmakers. One was called 'Inspired Gaming Group' and the other 'Global Draw' which has since been renamed 'S.G.Gaming.' The integral mechanism that runs the machine was made by a company called Playtech. Why did I need to know this? So I could email the entire board of all of the companies of course: their names were easily accessible on the internet.

After a lengthy wait I received a reply from the M.D. of Global Draw, and we regularly exchanged emails. I was pointing out that these machines were causing misery to so many, and that I was advocating a locking and unlocking device to be fitted to each one so that children and the vulnerable would be better protected. I recognised that people must be given freedom of choice, so suggesting a device that would stop children playing seemed to me an appropriate step. I felt that this was also something that could be realistically achieved. I had read that one of the founding principles of the Gambling Commission was to protect children and the vulnerable. I pointed out that in 2009 109,000 children had entered bookmakers, and in 2013 that number had risen to 588,000. These are the official figures as published by the Commission. By Law no person is allowed to enter a betting shop until they are 18.

A week or two later I was lying in bed and the name 'GamServe' came to mind, and straight away it made such sense to me. 'Gam' was short for 'gambling' and 'Serve' gave the message that we exist to serve those who are suffering as a result of gambling. I jumped of my bed and ran and told Phil and his wife Sandy, who were rather shocked, as they were in bed. I shouted from the bottom of the stairs. The next day I informed my friend Iain of the name and he began constructing the website. And so GamServe was born.

I then started to look at other ways to reach out to sufferers. For a large portion of my life I had been processed by the criminal justice system, and it suddenly struck me that there was no gambling programme ever offered to me while I was in prison. I did a great deal of research and I found out that the leading provider of drug and alcohol programmes in the UK prison system was an organisation called RAPT: "Rehabilitation Addicted Prisoners Trust." So to me the obvious thing to do was to approach them and see if they would be interested in incorporating a gambling programme into the prison system. So after sending numerous emails back and forth a meeting was arranged for January 14th 2014. Iain and I went to their offices in Vauxhall to meet with their development director. The meeting seemed to go well and we managed to represent our cause clearly, but there was no suggestion at that point that our requests would be put into motion. After half an hour it was clear that the meeting was drawing to an early close, but we left on the understanding that the organisation would be in touch. Unfortunately this has not been the case.

In February 2014 I went to the ICE exhibition with Iain. The exhibition is held in the Excel Centre in London. The whole place was filled with companies showing off the latest gadgets being used in the gambling industry, and as we looked for the Global Draw stall my heart sank as I saw the enormity of the task ahead. This place was filled with money and greed. I asked the woman at the stall that we had come to meet the M.D. She suspiciously looked us up and down but when I said that the appointment was pre-arranged she then told us to stand by some machines. About five minutes later he approached us and introduced himself. He showed us how the FOBTs worked and then proceeded to show us the new technology that had been developed for the machine, which (he was keen to point out) included better player protection. He had resisted my suggestion of a locking/unlocking device on the basis that this is the responsibility of the individual bookmakers.

As the day continued I noticed a stall marked 'The Gambling Commission.' I went across and introduced myself. At first it seemed that the compliance officer was wary of me and Iain, but some general chit chat seemed to put him at ease. I was interesting in finding out how many compliance officers policed the 10,000+ betting shops nationwide, and to my utter astonishment he said "40." He agreed that that wasn't anywhere near enough. Funding and resources are just not available, and people are suffering unnecessarily.

Just as we were about to leave the building despondent, in the corner I spotted an organisation called GamCare. I had read that they offered support to gambling addicts through one-to-one counselling over the internet, so I was eager to know more. As I approached a GamCare representative a woman blurted out "What do you want?" For a moment I thought I had misheard her, but no: that's what she said. No courtesy or manners, and that put me on edge. I began to say that I was interested in what they were doing when she interrupted me to say she couldn't talk to me. I made my excuses and left. I found out later that GamCare is funded by the gambling industry, which clearly raises questions over whose interests they are really looking after.

As I was leaving the Excel Centre that day I noticed that very few people were playing the machines, and that thought stayed with me for the rest of the day. That night as I was drifting to sleep that picture of no one playing the machines came back to mind, and the Holy Spirit showed me that the reason that no one was playing was that no money was being exchanged. The machines had credits on them so people could play, but no money was exchanged in any of the games. Money was the root of all this.

 I was now really starting to eat into my debt. I had been working so hard, but each and every night as I lay on my bed reading the Bible I would invite and welcome the Holy Spirit. I would feel such a warm sensation, especially around my chest and heart, and I then would drift peacefully to sleep. I began praying for words, pictures and prophesy, and for God to use me.

Then I began to look for articles on the internet about gambling crime, and this intrigued me. I read an article from the University of Georgia which pointed out that it is an average of six times more expensive to incarcerate someone for gambling crimes than to process their case through a gambling court. I had to know more, so I emailed the pioneer of gambling courts - a Court Judge. He replied to my email, and over the coming months and years he gave me support and advice. This advice is ongoing, and I recently asked him if he would write a piece on gambling courts for this book. This is included as Appendix A.

Weekends provided my best opportunity to concentrate on what I could do to bring to light all of the issues surrounding gambling. I was determined to be as resourceful as I could with my limited time. Having said that, I knew that it would take years for real change to take place. I decided I would not give up, and each and every day I called on Jesus to give me his strength to get through each day.

My next avenue was to contact Christian Vision for Men after listening to Carl Beech at St Pauls and again at New Wine. I also talked to the Executive Director of Ministry Support, and I told him a little of my story. He then contacted the editor of *Sorted* Magazine, and a journalist from that publication interviewed me. That led to the publishing of an article in *Sorted* in the autumn of 2013. Over the years *Sorted* has included several GamServe articles in the magazine free of charge.

At that point I had a strong sense of God's presence, and I was making a concerted effort to follow the lead of the Spirit. The next step was to contact the CVM team, so Iain and I went up to Chesterfield to meet with them. We discussed ways in which we could reach more people. I was able to give my story, and at the end of this one of the team prayed for us. These meetings became more regular, and at one of them the marketing and communications director of CVM suggested that I write a blog collecting my thoughts and experiences around gambling. I wrote my first blog on 16th April 2014. In the years that followed, CVM has supported me when I attended the summer conference called "The Gathering" in a field in Swindon. By this time I had a stall, a banner and some literature to distribute.

I asked CVM if they would also contribute to this book. A representative's reply is included as Appendix B.

It was towards the end of 2014 that Iain informed he would no longer support GamServe. This was a bit of a shock, but I wished him all the best for the future. We prayed about this situation and I was absolutely sure that I had to keep on moving forward, and I did so with total support from my adopted family. I needed no further encouragement.

It was shortly afterwards that Phil came across an article in the Salvation Army paper *War Cry*. It was about an ex-army major who had lost everything through gambling. His name was Justyn. I decided I would contact him. He had written a book called *Tails I Lose*, so I wrote to the publishers and asked them if he could contact me. We exchanged emails and arranged to meet up in London, where we discussed various gambling issues. He has an amazing story to tell, and we seemed to get on, which always helps. Some months later I asked him if he would be a trustee at GamServe, and he agreed. Justyn leads a recovery programme in his local church and he is also a speaker now with CVM. He has kindly offered his perspective on the issue of gambling, which can be found in Appendix C.

I once again went to New Wine in the July of 2014 and during one of the seminars I felt the Holy Spirit show me a man who was standing up to pray. The words that I was asked to give him were "Mercy triumphs over justice" from James 2:13. As I looked over at him I knew I should approach him, but for some reason I didn't, and the next day I saw the same man. Again I said nothing. The following day, whilst I was in the main marquee, I prayed that if this man was supposed to receive the message, he be in my line of vision as I lifted my head. Of course, he was, and I needed no more prompting. I went over to him and introduced myself, and asked him if I could pray for him. He said "Yes," and so I did. After I finished I gave him the words that I felt were for him. He gave me his card and asked me to keep in touch. We corresponded with each other on many different occasions, and he now fully supports the work of GamServe as part of the team. He is the ex-President of Shell International.

I started to make a habit of praying for people, prompted by the Spirit. I remember going to the Reading Carnival, and after I had prayed for another man he gave me his card. I searched for him on the internet to find out that he was the ex-chief inspector of New Scotland Yard: the highest ranking C.I.D. officer in the U.K. I would never have been able to get anywhere near him in the past, but what is impossible for man is possible for God. Not for the first time I was amazed at how God can open doors at just the right time.

At the following year's New Wine (an annual pilgrimage for me now) I had heard Carl Beech talking about giving things away like money or clothes, and he gave a few examples of what had happened to him. After his talk I went to the shop on site to get some food, and while I was standing in the queue a little boy asked me for some money for a good cause. At that point I felt the Holy Spirit prompt me to give all I had to him. I had £60 for the remainder of the week so I did not put any money into the bucket which was in his hand. This continued to play on my mind for months to come.

A few months passed by, and I was nearing my goal of paying off my £10,200 debt. I was so pleased that all of the hard work I had put in was nearing completion. I had £2010 in the bank and my debt was still around £3600. I had managed to go away for the weekend and it was on the journey home that I once again was prompted by the Holy Spirit, but this time the voice said that I was to give away the £2000 that I had in the bank. When I returned home I wrote a cheque for £2000 and gave it away. I told Phil what I had done. With my best interests at heart, he asked whether I was really sure. I was. By July 2014 I was debt free. The credit card expiry date has now passed and I intend never to use one again. In those months I continued to write articles about gambling, which were published in local, county and national newspapers. I was also able to talk on local, county and national radio.

I decided that if I was ever to approach the government I had to do rigourous research and present solid evidence, so an idea came to mind: a project to see how gambling impacted family, friends and colleagues of a problem gambler. I had read that an average of ten people are affected for each gambling addict, and if I could gather research and evidence this would show that a greater proportion of people are being affected than the 0.6% of the population that the gambling commission claim. With that in mind I decided that I would ring Oxford University to see if anyone could help me to put together a survey, which I hoped would have academic approval.

They passed me on to Bangor University, who passed me on to Goldsmiths University. After playing the proverbial hot potato, I reached a woman who passed me on to Birmingham University to talk to a Professor there. I had reached the centre of the academic labyrinth. After over one hour on the phone I had finally tracked down someone who might be able to help me. He said to me "Do you know what day it is?" and I replied "It's Friday." It turned out he had Friday afternoons off, and that on this particular Friday he was about to embark on a two week holiday. I think I audibly groaned, but then he said "Email me today with what you want, questions for survey etc." So I did, and by the end of that day he had given me his academic approval for the survey.

With the help of Phil the Gambling Impact Survey was published on the GamServe website within a year. I approached CVM and they promoted the survey on their website. *Sorted Magazine* also promoted it, and after talking to the Aylesbury Church Network they promoted the survey too. I was able to talk about the survey and give my story of being a gambler on Mix96 and BBC3Counties Radio, and I was also interviewed by Adrian Chiles on BBC Radio 5Live on the subject of gambling in prisons. The results of the survey were as follows are included as Appendix D.

After corresponding with an organisation called Christian Action Research & Education (CARE) Phil and I were invited to their offices in Westminster. We were warmly welcomed and invited to a participate in a buffet lunch. Present at this meeting were Dan, Nola and Lyndon, and we had the opportunity to explain our mission, vision and goals. Our meeting went well, and we have stayed in contact. CARE's Parliamentary Affairs Spokesman has kindly offered an article on gambling from this charity's perspective, which is included as Appendix E.

On the 22nd June 2015 I was invited to go to Portcullis House in Westminster to talk to my MP John Howell. I had been communicating with him for over two years, raising the concerns that I had over gambling related issues. So on that day I put on my best (only) suit and travelled to London. As I left the station an impressive sight greeted me: Big Ben. I arrived early so I took a stroll down Whitehall past the gates of 10 Downing Street, and I snuck a quick peek into the banqueting house.

Then I backtracked to Portcullis House for the meeting. As I entered the building security was tight. I had to remove my belt and any metal objects on my body and put them in a tray which was then scanned through an x-ray machine at the end of the conveyer belt. As I removed my belt and buckled up my trousers I looked up and saw that a police officer with a gun was standing by. I then reported to reception where the receptionist instructed me to take a seat. Within five minutes I was called by another member of staff who then took me through a glass door into a lift and down a corridor where John's office was. As we entered the room John stood up behind his desk and shook my hand. I was in his office for no more than 25 minutes, and in that time I was able to ask him about a 9pm watershed on gambling advertisement, the notion of an introduction of gambling courts in the UK, and the possibility of specific gambling programmes to be introduced into the prison system. John said very little, but he listened. I returned home hopeful that something would be done.

In August 2015 I returned for my annual holiday to New Wine, and as usual I felt inspired and refreshed after a week of listening to inspirational speakers. On one night I was able to give my story on New Wine Radio. This lasted around an hour, and I was later able to upload that talk to the GamServe website. The very next day I received a text from the radio team asking me whether I would be willing to talk to a man who had heard the backend of my story the night before. How could I turn down a request as cryptic as that?

He was the head of innovation and modernisation for the courts and tribunal service. I was astonished; this man potentially had direct contact with the policy makers. I talked to him for about thirty minutes and I then had the opportunity to pray for him and he prayed for me. I have been in contact with him since.

From my initial research I was beginning to understand how the gambling industry worked, and more and more doors were being opened to me. I had built up relationships with a Court Judge in America, a member of the Select Committee for Media, Culture and Sport, a university lead Professor, the list of contacts goes on and on. When Ian left Justyn became a Trustee and Adam Lomas began to support GamServe. We now have a website, and the number of people we can reach has increased as a result.

Words, Healings and Dreams.

'Follow the way of love and eagerly desire spiritual gifts, especially the gifts of prophecy.' 1 Corinthians 14:1

I would like to step back from the story at this point. Some people might not believe or understand this chapter. It is an account of events that only I have experienced, so I would not expect you to buy into it without any doubts. All that I would ask is that you approach what I am saying with an open mind. Over a period of five years starting in 2010 I saw and heard the following dreams and visions.

The Dark Presence

While I was asleep I suddenly became aware of a dark presence in my bedroom, and the very hairs on the back of my neck stood on end. I felt this evil presence jump on my back and as it was holding me down I heard the words "How did he get under our radar?" I was beginning to struggle for breath and with that I murmured "Help me Lord" and immediately the dark presence left the bedroom. Needless to say I had an uncomfortable night. To this day I do not know what the words meant.

The Winged Dream

I found myself going down a corridor approaching a set of doors which were open. I continued through the open doors and as I turned around to close them I heard a voice saying "Don't close the doors. The river of life flows through here." I instantly felt God's glory and Love, and the words "Go and collect my children" followed. I then began to move back along the corridor, and as I looked to my left and right I saw familiar faces, some praying, some laughing and jumping up and down. The laughter seemed to be bursting out of them. As I opened my arms they began to run towards me, and I instinctively opened my arms to embrace them. At that moment I looked down to close my fingers. To my utter astonishment and bemusement my arms had become wings.

I then set off towards to the end of the corridor and another set of doors were opened. As I looked up I could see dark clouds ahead, but as I approached they disappeared into the far distance, out of sight and out of mind. I then found myself in the clouds, flying, and as I looked down I could see all of the familiar faces I had met in the corridor. There were strangers too, and I collected them under my wings and gently placed them with the people I knew. This I continued to do, over and over. And then it dawned on me that I had a purpose, and people needed help.

The Lion Dreams

I was back in the form of a child. I felt safe and secure, burying my face deep into the mane of a lion, which I found myself riding. Eventually I got off the lion onto firm ground, and I then saw our Lord. I took hold of his hand, knelt to pick a flower and gave it God. This dream was repeated some time later, when the lion took me to a place in which I felt such an overwhelming sense of love, peace and joy. Again I felt God's glory on my face and in my body and I heard the words "I am pleased." Another time I dreamt I was in Heaven. To my right the Lord was addressing a congregation, and at that point I felt total and indescribable love.

A Prompting to Obey

I was at home, lying on the sofa, feeling very sorry for myself. I had aches and pains all over, feeling as though I was coming down with something. As I flicked through the Freeview channels the words "Deeds go to town" struck me. At that point I felt prompted by the Holy Spirit to get up and go to town, to which I responded "I can't. I am feeling terrible!" At that precise moment some words came to me from the Bible: "Why do you call me Lord, Lord, and do not do what I say?" Mark, the assistant pastor had sent me those exact words in a text message the day before. I needed no more prompting, so I got up and put my trousers on top of my pyjamas. I left the house and walked into Aylesbury. Nothing happened. Nothing at all. No one asked me any questions, nor did I feel prompted to approach anyone, and so I returned home. About an hour and a half later, feeling absolutely exhausted, even worse than before, I went straight back to the sofa and blurted out "Lord, why?" And I felt the Holy Spirit say "Obedience. Well done." With that I fell asleep. I later discovered that the words on the Freeview menu read ' Mr Deeds Goes to Town.' But by then the deed was done.

***

Christians are encouraged to step out of our comfort zone and to take risks, to see where God leads us. Here are just a few accounts of times I have steeped out in faith in this way. It usually starts with a request. I simply ask if someone would like prayer, and then see what God wants to do. The gentleness of the approach is essential. Prophecy may involve predicting future events, but its main purpose is to communicate God's message to people, providing insight, warning, correction and encouragement. Any names in this section have been changed.

The provision prayer

I felt a strong conviction to pray for prosperity in my workplace. During the recession, lots of factories were going out of business, but our factory went through an unprecedented period of prosperity and expansion. We got new machines and new employees, and business actually improved. Before long I was distributing Bibles and quietly praying for guys who approached me with stiff necks and bad backs; many of whom were healed overnight. During the years that followed I frequently asked them whether they were reading the Bibles that I had distributed. Some had, and some were insistent that they would get round to it. I always said "I don't know everything but if you need help or need something explained just ask." Some did and others did not. I have found over the years that a lot of people will just watch you to assess whether or not you are the real deal. I suppose it's about walking the walk, being known for your actions and deeds.

The Hearing Prayer

I was attending an evening service at New Wine. Towards the end a call was made for people to come forward for prayer. On these occasions I ask the Holy Spirit to guide me. I stayed at the back of the marquee waiting for the Holy Spirit to prompt me. A tall man attracted my attention and I knew it was him that I was going to approach. I asked him whether there was anything he would like prayer for. "No," he replied.

"Are you sure?"

His face shifted. "Well, I do have trouble hearing." then I
noticed that he had hearing aids in his ears. I said "Let me
pray for healing for your ears but, remember it is Jesus that
heals not me." He nodded. Then when I was praying for
him I had a strong sense that I should blow in his ear, so I
got on my tiptoes (he was very tall, as I have mentioned.)
The next morning I was at the back of the marquee and I
had my head down and a man got on the main stage in front
of 3000 people and said this: "Last night a man prayed for
my ears, and another man prayed for me this morning." He
then held out the hearing aids and pronounced that he
would not be needing them anymore. He could hear
perfectly without them. This was all caught on film.

The Ticket Inspector

I was on the train as the ticket inspector approached. I felt
the Holy Spirit prompt me to tell her that Jesus loved her. A
picture came into my head that I felt applied to her. This
picture was of her playing on a little scooter. As she got to
me, she asked me for my ticket and I asked her "Do you go
to church?" She said "No I never have done." I then asked
whether she had a small scooter that she played on. She
looked at me and said "How did you know that?" I then
assured her: "I want you to know that Jesus loves you. If
the scooter had been a coincidence, it is hard to explain
away what she said next. She informed me that I was the
second person to tell her that today. I said "I think Jesus is
reaching out to you." She smiled and continued up the
carriage.

Crime in the Cafe

I was in a queue waiting to get a cup of coffee, and as I looked over I could see a woman sitting down. For no obvious reason I could see the word 'CRIME' written across the back of her neck. I felt prompted to go over and pray for her. I asked her "Are you a police officer?" and she replied "No." She said that I could pray for her, and while I was praying I asked whether the word 'crime' meant anything to her. Again she denied it, so I continued to pray. Then I was prompted to ask again so I stopped and again she said that the word meant nothing to her. Upon the fourth time of asking she looked at me completely startled, and it struck her. "Oh, my job is as a biological forensic scientist and I work for the university. I work with crime." I was able to continue to pray for this woman. She informed me that she was not sure if she should stay at this place of work, or move to another job. I prayed into this situation with her.

Sam

I met Sam in the coffee shop and we started to talk about most things. He told me that he was having treatment for cancer and I asked him whether he believed in God. He told me that he didn't. Over the next two months we seemed to bump in to each other lots of times. I had plenty of opportunities to tell him about Jesus, and one day I said "You know Sam, I believe that God won't just force entry into your heart, but I do believe that he can send people around to gently let you know he's there." I had a text from Sam's wife two weeks later saying that he had died in hospital. I don't know if he gave his life to Jesus but I do know that I was obedient and faithful in telling Sam about our Lord.

On two different occasions whilst I was attending a Vineyard evening service I have experienced visions.

The First Vision.

I would guess that there were about 60-70 people present, and it was whilst we were worshiping and I had my eyes closed that this happened. I suddenly found myself able to see objects in front of me without opening my eyes, as clearly as I could see them with my eyes wide open. This often happens when I am communicating with the Holy Spirit.

In the distance I could make out the figure of a man, and as I approached the figure became clearer. We were in mid-air and as I got close the scene before me unfolded. The man was dressed in a long pure-white robe. He had a beard, but my eyes were drawn to the tassel that was around his waist. It had the most intricately woven knot and my gaze seemed to be transfixed by this knot. It hung from the right side of his waist. Then I felt myself being drawn away from the scene, and from a distance I observed as the man opened both of his hands and held them out. Thousands and thousands of birds came from his hands and began to fill the sky. The scene that I had witnessed finished and I opened my eyes. When we had finished worshipping the senior pastor asked whether anyone had any pictures or words that they felt that they would like to share. I responded that I had seen a man with his hands open and birds emerging. I did not go into any great detail, but the senior pastor also said that he got a picture of birds coming out of hands.

The Second Vision

This also took place during the evening service on a Sunday, and I would guess that over a hundred people were in attendance. With my eyes wide open a picture began to form before my very eyes. The colour of the picture that was forming was green, and I could make out that it was an open sack - the kind that you see farmers put their potatoes in. I did not understand what this meant, so I said "What is this?" Immediately the word "Barley" was drawn across the open sack. Then the vision ended.

***

There were other occasions when unusual things happened. Again I was worshiping, standing at the front of the auditorium having been prompted by the Holy Spirit that this was where I should sit. About ten minutes into the worship session I heard a whisper in my ear. It said I should take ten steps forward, turn around, keep my head held high and return to my seat. And so, after a little hesitation this is what I did. Then I continued to worship. When the singing had finished I felt the presence of God and immediately I opened my arms open wide and the Holy Spirit prompted me to speak. The words flowed from me, and in front of everyone I said "There is a sandstorm that is going to emerge from the east and sweep across Europe." Then that was it and the service continued.

As I was walking home from work one night I was just about home when I felt something touch my right shoulder. I immediately began to stagger, and I began swaying from side to side. I did not feel afraid but I did feel extremely drunk, and as I approached the front door and took the key from my pocket I had to balance myself by leaning on the left hand side of the frame. After a few attempts I got the key into the lock and opened the door. I shouted for Phil and Sandy as I entered the house but they were not at home, and I then went into the living room and collapsed onto the sofa. Within ten minutes the feeling of being drunk left and I was able to have a shower and get changed. Sometime later I told Phil and Sandy what had happened. This feeling of being drunk and swaying happened to me on two other occasions but to a lesser degree. I even went to the doctors and explained what happened and they could come up with no logical reason for it.

Later on when I was reading the Bible I felt that I was shown that I had been touched by the archangel Michael. Michael is an exceptionally strong angel who protects and defends people who love God. No matter what sort of situations you find yourself in Michael will give you the necessary courage and strength to deal with it.

One day I was at work as usual and as I looked to my right I saw what I can only explain was what looked like a big locust. It took my breath away, passing right in front of my eyes, and as I looked left I could see one of my work colleagues bent over. It went right above his head. He did not move at all, and as I watched it, it approached another of my colleagues who was working on the saw. It flew right by him and then turned right and disappeared. Not one of my colleagues saw it and you might be asking yourself "Why did you not shout out and tell anyone?" The reason is that I was dumbstruck; completely unable to communicate what I was witnessing to others around me. It was some time later that I told my senior pastor and assistant pastor what had happened. During the whole of this time I was receiving what I was praying for: words, pictures and prophesy.

One morning I was cleaning the church when I saw a picture and was given words for one of the senior pastors. I waited for an opportunity to share it with her, and that opportunity was not long in coming. I was cleaning the kitchen when she came in to make a cup of tea, so I said to her, "I feel as though I have a picture and words especially for you."

"Really?" she said, "Tell me."

" I saw a piece of fruit on top of your head and it was a strawberry."

And with that she laughed out loud and said "Ian, that is my favourite fruit. Then I told her the words God had given me: "The Lord is going to give you something sweet to digest."

"I wonder what that could be," she replied. Then she thanked me for being obedient to the prompting. Some months later the Vineyard was to become one of the host churches for the national conference. Maybe this was the sweet thing to digest. Several times I have been given pictures for the senior leadership and I have faithfully told the relevant people.

There are so many more dreams and experiences. I am not seeking attention; these are all to show you that if you are obedient and faithful and willing, with an open heart to step out in faith, God will never let you down.

Now I am aware of these things, I feel that it is my responsibility to share them:

"But the one who does not know and does things deserving punishment will be beaten with few blows. From everyone who has been given much, much will be demanded; and from the one who has been entrusted with much, much more will be asked."

If you are reading this and you are thinking that you would like to know more about Jesus I would suggest that CVM and New Wine are really good events to go to, even if you want to just look or explore further.

Actions and Consequences

Reflecting on my own experiences, I will now outline a typical route a gambler might take. It does not exemplify every case, but should give a general idea of the risks and measures a problem gambler is likely to take, and the impact it may have on others.

A Typical Route

Gambling was only recognised as an addiction in 2013 by the Diagnostic and Statistical Manual on Mental Disorders.

Gambling is fuelled by money: that is the drug. The insatiable pursuit of this drug is the addiction. A gambler will exhaust all avenues to obtain cash. This is an example of a typical route:

1. Overdrafts- This is the first option when spending becomes unmanageable.
2. Payday loans: These carry high interest rates and potentially accelerate debt quickly.
3. Bank loans- One loan is never enough. An addict is likely to spend it all in a very short period of time and then take out another loan. The debt spirals.
4. Family and Friends- The gambler becomes convinced it will only be for a short time until they can afford to pay back the debt. When it becomes clear this isn't the case, trust is destroyed and families collapse.
5. Sell possessions- There is no limit as to what this might include.
6. Crime- This is the final, tragic resort and the police will inevitably come knocking.

While these methods for obtaining money are not always used in this order, it is common for all of them to be used at some point in a gambler's 'career.'

Emotional Consequences

1. Anxiety: Worry, unease and tension begin to affect the gambler.
2. Anger- The gambler becomes angry with the whole situation that they are in. The bookmakers are taking their money, and they may feel life has dealt them a bad card, as if they are a victim.
3. Irritability- Getting annoyed and irritable because of the situation. Deep down it is most likely the gambler knows who is really to blame, and this gives rise to guilt.
4. Depression- Gambling has suddenly lost its attraction. It's not fun anymore, and no doubt the gambler is in debt and all of this is getting them down. Debt mounts up and hope is lost.
5. Suicidal thoughts- This one is a shock when it arrives. If you are suffering from these thoughts, there is a list of organisations than can help. Find them on www.gamserve.org.uk.

A gambler must become an expert in telling lies. In fact, before long it becomes second nature, a reflex action. Gambling addiction is not just about losing money.

Impact on others

A gambling addiction is like a stone dropped into the water and the ripples affect not only the gambler, but those around them too. It follows that a gambler's mental and physical health will be affected, and it will nearly always go on to affect their emotional wellbeing, and consequently their relationships. This may lead to family breakdown, crime, and debt. Perhaps worst of all, children and young people may become gamblers if it becomes a way of life in their families. When behaviours are normalised, there is a risk that they will be 'inherited.'

In an interview with Harriet Harmen, the ex-Shadow Culture Secretary, she admitted the Labour Government was wrong to relax the gambling laws that had brought high-stakes gambling machines into Britain's bookmakers. She said that "It's not just ruining the high street, its ruining people's lives." This was the first time Ms Harman, who was in charge of Labour's gambling policy, had explicitly blamed the Labour government for the increase in gambling. "I have got the most heart-rending letters and emails and calls that I've ever had in 30 years of being an M.P. just saying, "Please, do something about this. It's ruined my life, it's ruined my family, it's really dangerous."

Not much has changed since then.

With the increase in access to social media it is much more easily accessible, and it is hard to see how things will improve. The more that the general population is exposed to gambling the more people will be affected. It is my concern that if the government doesn't act now and take this seriously we are going to see an explosion of people who become addicted to gambling. This will have an impact on the Police, Probation Service, Courts, Prisons and Mental Health Services throughout the country.

Consequences of Criminal Conviction

If an addiction does lead to crime, the following consequences are commonplace:

- Crimes which carry a sentence of over two and a half years are never wiped from the record. This means that potential employers are able to view the information for the rest of the offender's life
- Car insurance premiums become far higher
- Household insurance premiums are more expensive

Advertising

There is no doubt that the increase in gambling advertisement has had a huge impact on families, and we are finding that an ever increasing amount of people are coming forward and asking for help. That is why we are campaigning for a 9pm watershed on gambling advertisement. The hope is that this will protect children and the vulnerable.

Betknowmore

This organisation helps gambling addicts and those who are impacted by gambling at a grass roots level.

Epilogue

I am, at this moment, sitting having a cup of coffee. I have not gambled for nearly four years now. This is the longest period since I was sixteen, and I can say with certainty that I am not the same as I was. My life has been transformed. Romans 12:2 comes to mind, where Saint Paul urges the Roman Church "Do not conform any longer to the pattern of this world, but be transformed by the renewing of your mind."

I take another sip of my coffee, sitting in my armchair looking out of my window into the back garden which has been my view for nearly four years. I begin to reflect on the time that I have spent here and my thoughts are drawn to the unconditional love that I have witnessed and felt from my adoptive family. They opened their home to me not quiet knowing what they were taking on, trusting in God that it was the right thing to do. At times, especially at the beginning, they must have felt that they were being taken on a rollercoaster ride, such is the turbulent nature of the change that has taken place over the years.

Then I think of when I was a total wreck, not quiet knowing what lay ahead, deep in debt, struggling to comprehend what had happened and what was happening to me. And yet even in those dark, lonely times I knew that I was not alone. Jesus was not going to give up on me even during the times I did not know it. As the days, months and years have passed I have clung on to my Lord, but no one had told me that the journey would be an extremely difficult one. And yet without fail (usually when we least expect it) our Lord turns up. Even in our weakest moments he is with us.

This year has seen another blessing enter my life, and an answer to prayer. Pam was a friend of Phil and Sandy's daughter. They introduced me to her, and we initially got to know each other by seeing each other occasionally at weekends. Within a year we began to see much more of each other, and we got engaged, to be married on July 24th 2016. We are to be married in a Methodist church that Pam attended as a child, and that her parents still attend. I am so thrilled and excited. Pam also has a story to tell concerning gambling; one which she just recently revealed to me. She agreed to write it down and include it in this book:

Just £5. That is what it had cost me for the night out. Not bad as it included at least six games of bingo, plus food and drink. Although I didn't win a game, I felt like a winner. It had been a great night out with friends and had cost very little indeed. Over the coming weeks and months I was to find myself going back regularly. Sometimes with others, sometimes alone. It was fun. It was a way to win money (in theory), but mostly it was a way to combat the loneliness and boredom which otherwise threatened to consume my evenings after work.

It wasn't long before the lure of the fruit machines took hold of me. Initially I'd play on the 10p slots, moving up to 50p and £2. It was only a matter of months until I was moving around gaming shops, maxing my cards out at cash points and borrowing. Driving home from my job as a primary school teacher I would be faced with the glittering lights of the bingo establishment, and have to choose between the excitement offered there or a lonely evening watching TV. To begin with I thoroughly enjoyed the company at the bingo, and even when, after a very short time, I began going alone to play the machines, I loved the social side. People were friendly and chatty and non-judgemental. I also learned that if I played particular machines I would get free food and drink. This was a bonus!

After a few months I realised my bank balance was suffering greatly, but by now I was addicted. Gambling was no longer fun or exciting but a compulsion. There were two main reasons:

1. *I needed to feel part of a community in the evenings.*
2. *I desperately hoped to win some money back.*

It finally got to the stage where I could no longer afford to pay my bills. Being a teacher, it was relatively easy to get a bank loan for over £7000. On my statement it clearly stated I'd been taking cash from inside the bingo outlet but the banker asked no questions and I didn't offer any answers. I felt relieved when I got the loan, like I'd escaped danger. I knew I should stop gambling but once again the urge came over me and I lost most of the loan amount. I'm still paying off that loan now.

As soon as it stopped being fun I realised I had a problem, but it was an overwhelming sense of shame and guilt which prevented my seeking help. After all, I was a professional teacher and a practicing Christian. Surely I should've known better. As the guilt increased people asked me what was wrong, but I just couldn't admit it. Fortunately one day, a lovely couple from church met with me and I was

able to open up. It was so freeing! There was no judgement.
My Christian friends met with me over a few weeks and
encouraged me to accept the freedom of Christ rather than
the condemnation of the enemy. I am still in contact with
these people, and by the grace of God I have stayed free
from gambling.

I find it absolutely amazing that Pam and I are together.
Not only do we love each other but also we have been
through similar experiences, and no doubt we will be able
to support each other in the months and years ahead. Would
it not be something spectacular if we both could witness to
those who are suffering from gambling as a husband and
wife team working together? A new chapter in my life is
about to begin and Pam and I are soon to hand in our
notices at work and move to a new life in Nottinghamshire.
We are both taking a step of faith and trusting in God that
exciting times are ahead.

During the process of writing this book, I have been asked
about the nature and extent of support that is available to
women who suffer from gambling addiction. Personally I
have never seen any help out there for these addicts, but I
would suggest that common sense would dictate that with
the increase of gambling advertisement, women are clearly
being targeted by advertisers. One of the most prominent
examples of this is bingo. This is a relatively untapped
market for the gambling industry, and they are quick to
pounce and take full advantage.

I want to use our stories to reach out and bring hope to
those who are struggling with this terrible addiction, so that
they might learn from my many mistakes. It's only when

you speak out the truth and tell someone: then, and only then, will they be able to accept help. When I think back to how out of control and chaotic my life was, it strikes me that at this time of morning I would not always have been relaxing and sipping a coffee. I would have been in a pub looking at the back pages at the horse racing, or gambling on those fixed odds betting terminals. That's all over now, and it is Jesus who took it away. He has brought me this freedom.

I am all too aware that I still have freedom of choice, and with that in mind I must put safeguards in place so that I don't go down the road I most want to avoid. The Bible calls for this self control. The measures that I have put into place include always telling the truth, and being able to say the word 'no.' It's a powerful word, and extremely effective. I don't buy newspapers; if I want to know the news I look it up online so that I can avoid the back pages. I have let it be known at work that I don't gamble, so I am no longer asked about being part of a syndicate such as the lottery or football sweepstakes. I have a Freeview box so I can skip by any racing. I have no desire to know the winner of The Grand National, The Derby, The Oaks. These thoughts have all gone. Instead of scheming over where I am going to get money I have been able to start giving some away.

I don't know what lies ahead for me but I will put my trust in my God. Where I am led, I will follow. St Paul also says *'For it is with your heart that you believe and are justified, and it is with your mouth that you confess and are saved. As the scripture says, anyone who trusts in him will never be put to shame.'*

I pray that in the months and years ahead I would always honour god and that I would step out in faith, being obedient and faithful to God's prompting. I also hope that those who read this story would be open to looking at who Jesus was and what he did. He came for humanity, and in him is the forgiveness of sins, no matter what they might be.

As I turn my head to the right on my bedroom door is a poster that says this:

'For I know the plans I have for you declares the Lord , plans to prosper you and not to harm you, plans to give you a hope and a future. Then you will call upon me and come and pray to me and I will listen to you. You will seek me and find me when you seek me with all your heart.' I hope these words will continue to be true for me, as they were for Jeremiah all those thousands of years ago.

Phil recently said to me "Ian, you are a man of integrity and a man of God."

That will do for me.

Thank You

I first came across Christian Vision for Men at a 2012 conference called Courageous, and it was at this conference that the Holy Spirit spoke to me personally. After a few weeks I contacted CVM to see whether they would be interested in hearing my story. They were, and shortly after that the executive director contacted the editor of *Sorted Magazine*, and they ran a story in the September/October issue of the magazine entitled 'Take a gamble on God.'

I was then offered a space to write blogs on the CVM website, describing my experiences of gambling. To date I have written six blogs in which I have described not only my own experiences, but also how God has transformed me, and how I am stepping out in faith in all types of different circumstances.

About a year later I visited the offices of CVM in Chesterfield and I had the opportunity to explain what GamServe was doing and how I was called to reach out to those who are suffering with gambling addictions. Through this meeting and other communications GamServe became partners with CVM. Together with their associate charities I have found CVM to be extremely encouraging in giving me both practical support and advice. On many occasions I have been extremely grateful for their words of wisdom, especially during the more difficult challenges.

Thanks:

CVM: I want to say a big Thank you to all of the team at Christian Vision for Men. This movement certainly has a place in my heart, and I am praying that more men will be reached by their enthusiasm and sincerity in showing and revealing Jesus to those who are lost.

Gambling Reform Groups: I came across the gambling reform groups in 2015 when I visited London and I want to offer my thanks to those groups for listening to what I had to say, and of course for promoting the Gambling Impact Survey. I look forward to continued collaboration.

CARE: Thank you for your input in this book, and I am most grateful that you invited both Phil and I to your offices in Westminster. I hope that we stay in touch.

Mark: I appreciate your input and advice over the last three years. Keep on moving forward with Gambling Courts in the U.S.A.

Steve and _Sorted Magazine_: I appreciate all you have done for GamServe over the last three years and I am looking forward to meeting up at the next "The Gathering" in a field near Swindon.

John Howell M.P: I would like to say thank you for inviting me down to Westminster and giving me the opportunity to discuss gambling-related issues. I hope that conversation can continue.

Aylesbury Church Network: Thank you for giving me the opportunity to speak about gambling, and for backing the Gambling Impact Survey.

Aylesbury Vineyard: Thank you for allowing me to display GamServe cards and pamphlets, and for you support and encouragement over the years.

Professor Jim Orford, Birmingham University: Without your help and input the Gambling Impact Survey would have been nigh on impossible for me to implement. Thank you.

Johanna and Lisa: For sending me a specific gambling programme for prisons in the U.K, thank you.

Iain: I thank you for your encouragement and support during the early stages of setting up GamServe.

Justyn: I thank you for your input, and I am looking forward to continuing to work with you.

Tom: Without your input and advice, this book would have been a near impossibility to put together.

Frankie: Thank you for your input for this book, and for your friendship.

Pam: Thank you for loving me for who I am.

Phil & Sandy and My Adoptive Family: You have all been an inspiration and a constant encouragement to me and I am privileged to know you. You can count on it that you'll never really get rid of me. I love you all.

And to everyone else who has supported me on this journey I offer my sincere thanks. I hope that our efforts amount to real change.

Appendix A

Judge Mark G. Farrell- The Gambling Treatment Court Experience: A Struggle for Progress & Therapeutic Innovation in the Criminal Justice System

Against the backdrop of a steadily expanding commitment to the concept of Therapeutic Justice in the Criminal Justice System through Drug Treatment Courts, Community Courts, Mental Health Courts, Veterans Courts and Driving while Intoxicated Courts ,to name just the more highlighted examples ,there continues to exist an historically rooted and pervasive reluctance to acknowledge, let alone intervene with, serious gambling abuse or the addiction of pathological gambling as it relates to the commission of a criminal act.

This gaping hole and lack of any structure or interest to respond therapeutically to gambling in the American Legal System became the impetus for exploring a unique stand alone Court in Amherst NY in 2001 dedicated to therapeutic intervention where compulsive or pathological gambling was the genesis of criminal activity. The dichotomy of approach as between that prevalent in the therapeutic "Problem Solving" Courts related to drugs ,alcohol, mental health and Veterans issues and the distinctly punitive dealings with gambling defendants is rooted both societally and in the Courts on the belief that pathological gambling offenders are character flawed and deserving of only the application of punitive and deterrence based theories of punishment, as opposed to acknowledgement of a medical, disease based problem requiring therapeutic intervention. The general lack of favourable pleas offers by prosecutors and the application of generally more severe incarcerative sentences by the Courts are far more prevalent in the case of gambling addicted defendants than is routine, from this writers experience ,with drug addicted ,alcoholic or mentally ill criminal violators.

All of this being said, Gambling Treatment Court was initiated in the late summer of 2001 after the arraignment of almost two dozen defendants in less than a three week span with all of the offenders exhibiting various levels of clinical manifestations of addictive gambling symptoms without the clear presence of serious drug and/or alcohol abuse or addiction or with a distinct mental health diagnosis. It should be noted that this finding then did not, at that time, and does not today diminish our overall realization of the co-morbidity between drugs, alcohol, mental health and gambling. We applied the medical model, the existing Drug Court protocol we had been using for six years at that time, and sought outside expert assistance eventually concluding the presence of a gambling pathology as the primary causative factor in the criminal behavior. This population was clearly different and unique, deserving of a therapeutic judicial intervention in a separate setting, contractually based, judicially monitored, as in Drug Court, while committed to abstinence and focused on responsible and accountable recovery.

This endeavour was implemented and thereafter staffed by certified gambling treatment providers who were tasked with the mandate of authoring and providing the Court with regular written status reports on participants. Inpatient and Outpatient treatment facilities were recruited and utilized as additional available resources.

Consistent with the procedures operative in our "sister" Drug, Alcohol, Mental Health and Veterans "Problem Solving" Courts, defendants were clearly advised of expectations, had pled to the highest charged offense with a promise of either a serious reduction of the charge or dismissal upon graduation as a motivating factor and were thereafter mandated to multifaceted individually structured inpatient or outpatient treatment regimens with regular progress reporting dates before the Court. On these docketed dates, the participants were/are either rewarded for positive performance, abstinence and integrity or sanctioned in various ways including possibly short periods of incarceration, for lack of adherence to their individually tailored program of recovery or their lack of integrity and repetitive relapses.

As the Court matured, cognitive behavioural components, as well as Gamblers Anonymous, Gam-Anon, re-education therapy, Replacement Addiction sessions, Vocational training, drug and alcohol treatment, and mental health referrals became standard requirements for program processing and completion.

Identification, initial screening and follow up compliance have been the greatest challenges as the Court enters its 15th year.

Interest in this type of judicial intervention around the United States and the World, in terms of replication, has grown markedly but real expansion is still a challenge as the public at large, political, legislative, policy making, judicial and prosecutorial representatives still struggle with application of the disease based model to this "addiction" as opposed to applying the "character flaw" approach that bespeaks little chance for both individual recovery and real societal benefit. The struggle continues...

Appendix B
Nathan Blackaby, Executive Director of Ministry CVM

I joined the CVM team in 2014 after having worked as a Chaplain to a drug rehabilitation project for men in Brazil and then in Church planting and pastoring in Essex. It is such a privilege to serve with an amazing team of really focused people, what are they focused on? Well!

CVM started about 20+ years ago and over that time has developed and built upon one core theme, to introduce men to Jesus. Our vision is to encourage, equip and inspire men to be the Christ follower they know they need to be and build a movement that will see 1,000,000 men and then some turn to Jesus as their captain, brother, rescuer and friend.

All around us we can see the decline of men attending church and the impact this is having on the generations to come so as a movement we fight for this to be a story of the past. With cutting edge, quality resources for every stage of a man's journey with Jesus, CVM is equipping and train at specific days and events and in collaboration with over 500 Christian men's groups registered with us we are taking ground!

Developed within CVM is a 4 level evangelism strategy that we have seen prove to be effective, in building strong friendships between men and enabling an honest and clear presentation of Jesus and his calling on the hearts of men today.

CVM present a clear evangelistic message in all we do, but we also call out and challenge the issue in life that blunt, numb and dismantle faith in Jesus for men.

In addition to the regular events, training days, church days and resources, CVM run an annual men's festival called the Gathering. This festival has grown incredibly over the last 5 years and we now expect 2,000 men and more each year. The event is a lot of fun, with cars, bikes, axe throwing and beer. However, behind all the fun is something that drives all of the team at CVM, the Gathering is an evangelistic event and this is central in the worship, teaching and gospel that is presented. We use events like the Gathering and more to call men from their caves and into the most incredible life of following Jesus Christ our King, that's what CVM are all about.

Appendix C

Justyn Rees Larcombe, author and speaker.

Problematic Gambling Provision in the UK

Gambling addiction is not a well understood addiction. It was only officially recognised and classed as a pathological medical condition in 2013.

The NHS has one clinic based in Fulham. Led by Dr Henrietta Bowden-Jones, The National Problem Gambling Clinic treats 1,000 people each year, but this is just the tip of the iceberg.

The industry, through a levy, fund GamCare. An organisation which offers free advice through national helplines and a network of counsellors for those who are struggling. However, due to their funding being entirely from the gambling industry, it has been suggested that the provision the offer could contribute to the relative lack of research into the extent of the problem.

The fact that the fastest growing age group calling these helplines is the 16 to 24 year olds would suggest that the problem is a growing one. A recent article in The Times (17th Feb 2016), suggested that the number of people who suffer a pathological addiction in the UK has increased significantly to much more than 550,000. The figure was last recorded in 2010 at 450,000. For every one problem gambler there are perhaps 10 people adversely affected by the actions of the addict.

It is therefore surprising that the most effective treatment and recovery pathway is an independent self-funded organisation called Gamblers Anonymous (GA). GA meetings take place up and down the country, but the number of groups is not high. For example, in Kent, one of the largest counties in the UK, there are only three groups who meet each week.

GA has helped and continues to help many and is free to all.

For those who can pay for treatment, there are specialist addiction counsellors and private clinics who offer a service. An example is the Harley Street based Cognacity Group. However, by the time an individual has developed a pathological addiction to gambling, they are unlikely to be able to afford expensive and often, long term, treatment for their addiction.

There are also a number of charities who have been established to raise awareness of the issue and offer training to those who deal with at risk groups such as youth, offenders and other vulnerable groups. EPIC Risk Management also offer education and awareness training as well as arranging intervention and recovery pathways for corporate organisations, the military, professional sport and the prison sector.

However, in summary, I believe that the provision of effective and accessible treatment for this condition is yet to catch up with the scale of the issue and the gap is widening. It will continue to do so unless there is significant social change in our society and the proliferation of advertising and lack of education from a young age is addressed.

Appendix D

Ian Bartlett, Gamserve

The Gambling Impact Survey Summary

More than 100 people completed the survey, with over 92% of them being men. Over 30% of the respondents had been impacted by a close family member with a gambling problem in the last 12 months, whilst the rest had been involved with someone outside the family in the last 12 months who gambled.

Of those with a close family member who gambled, over 70% experienced anger, confusion, anxiety and financial difficulty, while 60% said that they sometimes encountered physical stress, depression and loneliness and over half said that they felt ashamed, scared and betrayed.

Interestingly when you realise that the respondents were mainly men, 50% of those with close family members who gambled, said that they had suffered emotional abuse from the gambler and nearly half of these said it developed into physical abuse.

The survey revealed that family breakup is a key impact of gambling and over 50% of those with a gambler in the family experience family break-up, almost half of which ended in divorce.

Over 90% of all respondent believed that there should be a 9:00pm watershed on gambling advertising on TV.

Can gambling really be classified as an entertainment?

The Survey Analysis

Knowing someone with a gambling problem: the results of an online survey

The analysis of the Gambling Impact Survey were produced by Professor Jim Orford of Birmingham University.

Respondents of the Survey
Anyone who was the spouse, relative or friend of a problem gambler was invited to take part.
There were 105 respondents: 97 male, 8 female
Ages:
18-24 – 2
25-34 – 6
35-44 – 22
45-54 – 33
55-64 – 29
64 or over – 13

9 made it clear in comments after particular questions or at the end that they did not know anyone with a gambling problem, so they have been excluded from the analysis.

32 said they know a close family member with a gambling problem in the last 12 months.

22 said they know either a friend (10) or a work colleague or someone at school or college (10) or a more distant relative (2) with a gambling problem in the last 12 months.

42 said they know someone else with a gambling problem in the last 12 months.

The results for the last of those two groups were very similar, so they have been combined into one group of others.

Experiences as a result of that person's gambling

The table below shows the percentages of the two groups who reported each experience 'sometimes' or 'often' (and in brackets just the percentages reporting each experience 'often'). The 14 experiences are ordered from those with highest scores to those with the lowest for the Knows a close family member group

	Know a close family member N=32 Experienced at least sometimes (often)	Others N=64 Experienced at least sometimes (often)
Anxious	78.1 (65.6)	17.2 (9.4)
Angry	84.4 (46.9)	26.6 (4.7)
Confused	78.1 (43.8)	20.3 (7.8)
Financial difficulties	71.9 (53.1)	6.3 (4.7)
Physical stress	65.6 (46.9)	0.0 (4.7)
Depressed	68.7 (31.3)	6.3 (3.1)
Burnt out	65.6 (37.5)	0.0 (7.8)
Scared	53.1 (43.8)	4.7 (1.6)
Lonely	62.5 (40.6)	4.7 (1.6)
Betrayed	56.2 (28.1)	9.4 (7.8)
Ashamed	53.1 (18.8)	4.7 (1.6)
Hassled for money	46.9 (28.1)	12.5 (4.7)
Emotional abuse	50.0 (18.8)	1.6 (0.0)
Physical abuse	21.9 (6.3)	0.0 (0.0)

Adding up each person's scores for those 14 items (each item scored: often 3; sometimes 2; occasionally 1; never 0) produces the following results:

Those who know a close family member (N=32): mean score 24.3, standard deviation 10.7, range 1-38, median 27

Others (N=64): mean score 5.4, standard deviation 6.3, range 0-30, median 2/3

Other results:

Family break-up. Those who know a close family member - 18 (56.3%); Others - 5 (7.8%)

Divorce. Those who know a close family member - 8 (25.0%); Others -3 (4.7%)

In favour of a 9 pm watershed for TV gambling advertising. Those who know a close family member - 29 (90.6%); Others - 62 (96.9%)

The chart below shows the distribution of those total scores for the two groups: Those who know a close family member (Family); and Others.

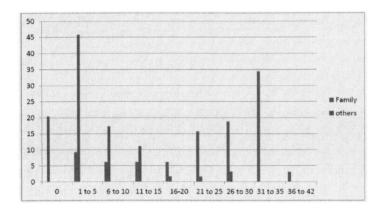

The X-Axis represents the total scored, which would be 42 if all the questions were answered as "Often", while the Y-Axis is the total number of respondents in that group.

Appendix E
Dr Dan Boucher, parliamentary affairs spokesman,
CARE

CARE'S Fight for Better Protections for Problem Gamblers

Problem gambling is devastating both for those concerned and their families. It leaves in its wake a trail of social destruction that society cannot afford to ignore. CARE (Christian, Action, Research and Education) engages with this challenge as a public policy charity with the objective of pressing the Government to introduce more robust legal and policy provisions to protect problem gamblers.

Online Gambling

Our initial point of concern was online gambling. Unlike terrestrial gambling, online gambling can be accessed 24/7. Moreover, the protections that arise out of the act of leaving the house, and family members asking where you are going, do not apply. Far from having to leave your house you do not even have to leave your own bedroom. Indeed, in our work in this area we have even become aware of a problem gambler who gambled secretly in bed next to his sleeping wife using an electronic device under the duvet so as not to wake her.

Our concerns were compounded when dealing with online gambling as a result of the fact that one of the main protections offered problem gambling 'self-exclusion' is not provided in a credible manner to those who gamble online. While it is possible that on a strong day a problem gambler could visit the 6 betting shops in his town and cut himself off from terrestrial gambling opportunities in his local community by self-excluding for, say, the next 6 months so he can get help, the same protection is not afforded to online problem gamblers. The truth is that once you have self-excluded from 6 gambling web sites that you can access from your bedroom, there are still hundreds of other sites equally available in your bedroom and it is impossible for anyone to physically self-exclude from them all. As one on-line problem gambler said to us, 'I can self-exclude, but then there are always other sites.'

Moreover, while the 2005 Gambling Act was cognisant of the fact that gambling sites can be accessed in the UK that are not located in this country and do not have a UK Gambling Commission license, it only sought to engage with suppliers beyond the UK by creating a white list of jurisdictions whose regulatory regimes it deemed sufficiently robust to permit them to advertise in the UK. It did precisely nothing, however, to prevent online gambling sites that were not based in white listed jurisdictions from selling their services to UK customers. Indeed, the 2005 Gambling Act weakened direct UK regulation by creating an incentive for online gambling companies located in the UK, and thus subject to the full regulation of the Gambling Commission, to relocate to white listed jurisdictions with lower tax rates, where they would be free of the UK Gambling Commission.

The Government recognised that its Act had created a problem and in early 2010 decided to consult about the best way forward. Eventually the Gambling (Licensing and Advertising) Bill emerged in 2013. It abolished the system of white listed jurisdictions requiring that henceforth any online gambling provider wanting to access the UK Gambling market must secure a UK Gambling Commission license, a condition of which was being a UK tax payer. While this arrangement dealt with the tax issue, however, CARE was deeply concerned that it failed to address two other pressing problems:

In the first instance, in the same way that the previous arrangement did not prevent online gambling sites located in non-white-listed jurisdictions from selling to people in the UK, the new framework contained no provisions to prevent online gambling providers located outside the UK, and without a UK license, from selling to people in the UK. Not being able to advertise officially does not prevent sites from accessing the UK market, especially if they are offering good odds.

Second, we were concerned that while under the 2005 framework only sites located in the 31 white listed jurisdictions could advertise in the UK, under the new proposals, any provider located in any of the 183 + jurisdictions of the world could advertise if they secured a UK Gambling Commission license.

CARE responded to these two concerns by promoting two different amendments to the Gambling Bill, first as it was considered by the Commons and then as it was considered by the Lords.

In the first instance, we argued that without an enforcement mechanism to prevent unlicensed online gambling providers accessing the UK market, the Bill could not live up to its aspiration to enhance regulation and player protection. The amendment that we proposed placed a statutory obligation on Financial Transaction Providers requiring them not to process transactions between unlicensed online gambling providers and anyone in the UK.

In the second instance, we argued that it simply was not appropriate to dramatically widen the scope for online gambling advertising in the UK, with all that this would mean for problem gamblers, without addressing the anomaly that online problem gamblers are not afforded a credible form of self-exclusion. We promoted an amendment to the Bill that mandated the introduction of a multi-operator self-exclusion mechanism, on the basis of which a problem gambler need only self-exclude once and the terms of their self-exclusion should immediately apply to all other licensed gambling providers.

As the Bill passed through the House of Commons the Government firmly resisted both amendments. This did not stop Jim Shannon MP forcing a vote on self-exclusion. Although the Government won, the Opposition parties supported the amendment which received a very respectable 223 votes to 283 votes on 26 November 2013.

When the Bill entered the Lords the Government front bench adopted a similar approach at Second Reading and Committee Stage. Once the Bill had reached its Report Stage (4 March 2016), however, and Ministers could see that Peers took their concerns very seriously, the Government moved on both issues.

The Minister, Baroness Jolly, told Baroness Howe of Idlicote - who had tabled the amendment requiring Financial Transaction Providers not to process transactions with unlicensed providers - that the Government acknowledged the importance of the issue her amendment addressed. She explained that the Gambling Commission had now approached the Financial Transaction Providers and secured an agreement from them that going forward they would not process financial transactions between unlicensed providers and UK consumers. While Baroness Howe was delighted that at long last the Government had acknowledged the problem and taken action, she was not persuaded that the voluntary nature of the agreement with the Financial Transaction Providers sounded sufficiently robust. Mindful of this she argued that a statutory approach was required and she pressed her amendment to a division which she only just lost by 14 votes, 171 to 185.

Meanwhile, the Government told Lord Browne of Belmont, who had tabled the multi-operator self-exclusion mechanism amendment, that again, having previously refused to acknowledge the problem, they had now asked the Gambling Commission to consult on the introduction of this system and that they wanted it applied both online and offline. Mindful of this, Lord Browne withdrew his amendment and the Gambling Commission proceeded to consult.

Although neither amendment was accepted, they both highlighted serious problems as the Bill passed through the Commons and the Lords and eventually the Government was forced to concede that action was needed on both points. The Gambling Commission and the financial transaction providers have been working together on blocking illegal transactions and the Gambling Commission has consulted on, and is now working with the industry on, the introduction of multi-operator self-exclusion. It is doubtful that action would have been taken in either respect if it was not for the parliamentarians who spoke up so eloquently for better protections for the vulnerable as the legislation was scrutinised by Parliament. CARE is particularly grateful in this regard for the work of Jim Shannon MP, Clive Efford MP, Baroness Howe of Idllicote and Lord Browne of Belmont.

Fixed Odds Betting Terminals

Having initially engaged with online gambling, CARE has more recently become involved with pressing for better regulation of the most addictive form of terrestrial gambling, Fixed Odd Betting Terminals. Often described as the crack cocaine of gambling, FOBTs present a unique challenge arising out of the way in which they combine high stakes with a very high speed of play which means that it is possible for people to lose a lot of money very quickly, up to £18,000 per hour. The most reliable data suggests that as many as 37% of those who use FOBTs regularly have a problem, an extraordinary attrition rate that cannot be allowed to go unchallenged. FOBT use has been linked to: family breakdown, suicide, anti-social behaviour and money laundering.

The consensus amongst a range of bodies ranging from 93 local authorities who have petitioned the Government to change the law, the Campaign for Fairer Gambling and ourselves is that the most appropriate policy solution is to reduce the maximum stake per spin on FOBTs from £100 to £2. We have worked closely with Lord Clement Jones on developing his Gambling Private Members Bill that has precisely this effect. The Bill had its Second Reading on 11 March 2016 and, whilst the Government has not amended its position in any way, CARE was encouraged that the Bill provided the opportunity for a debate in which practically all contributors backed the Bill apart from the Minister. It also provided the opportunity for a former chairman of the bookies Paddy Power to write a very powerful opinion piece in favour of the Bill in the Times. Going forward CARE will continue to make the case for reducing the maximum stake per spin on FOBTs to £2 per spin.

Conclusion

Although CARE's work with parliamentarians to fight for better protections for problem gamblers has not yet resulted in the development of new legislation, it has resulted in new Government policies. Our work in this area demonstrates how sustained engagement with the Government over a period of time on an issue can generate real change. We are encouraged by the progress that has been made but there is still a great deal to do, especially with respect to FOBTs in relation to which the case for change is now, in our view, overwhelming.

Ian Bartlett is the founder of GamServe. He campaigns to change the laws and mindsets surrounding gambling in order to better protect the young and vulnerable from developing a gambling addiction.

Ian can be contacted at: ianfortyyears@gmailcom

Printed in Great Britain
by Amazon